the sweet life

the sweet life

Find Passion, Embrace Fear, and
Create Success on Your Own Terms

dulce candy ruiz

AVERY

An imprint of Penguin Random House LLC
375 Hudson Street
New York, New York 10014

LIBRARY OF CONGRESS CATALOGING-IN-PUBLICATION DATA

Ruiz, Dulce Candy, 1987–
The sweet life : find passion, embrace fear, and create success on your own terms /
Dulce Candy Ruiz.
pages cm
ISBN 978-1-59240-950-1 (hardback)
1. Ruiz, Dulce Candy, 1987– 2. Makeup artists—United States—Biography.
3. Beauty, Personal. 4. Fashion. 5. Success.
6. Celebrities—Miscellanea. I. Title.
TT955.R85A3 2015
646.7'2092—dc23
[B]
2015007533

Printed in the United States of America

1 3 5 7 9 10 8 6 4 2

Set in Palatino LT STD · *Designed by Elke Sigal*

Contents

contents

Introduction

Hi, guys! I can't even begin to tell you how excited I am to share this book with all of you. Whether you've stuck by me from day one—when I was still in the military, posting shaky YouTube videos out of my tiny bedroom—or recently became a part of my online community or simply picked up this book because you were intrigued by the cover (it's pretty cute, huh?), I want to thank you from the bottom of my heart for embarking on this journey with me.

"Dulce Candy"—the name my very imaginative parents gave me—translates to "sweet candy" in Spanish. Sure, it gets a few giggles now and again, but I wouldn't change it for the world. I consider my name a constant reminder to never ever lose sight of the sweet things in my life. One of the absolute sweetest is the support of the viewers who keep coming back to my YouTube channel day after day. It's all the proof I need that my whirlwind of a life has taken me exactly where I need to be.

Here's what's weird: Though I've loved everything about makeup—the dizzying spectrum of colors, the pretty packages, that instantly recognizable scent—long before YouTube was invented, I never actually planned on becoming a vlogger, or a beauty guru for that matter. In fact, for a long time I didn't think I'd become much of anything. Just like so many of us, I went through some tough times, the toughest of which were in high school. As you'll soon find out, joining the military after graduating was a transformative experience. It set me on a path that would eventually shape me into the woman I am today. A woman who knows her strengths yet learns from her weaknesses. A woman who is her own boss yet still understands the power of teamwork. A woman who came out on top despite the odds.

My job has given me opportunities to work with incredible brands like L'Oréal, CoverGirl, and Virgin America. My work has been recognized by major publications (thanks, *Women's Wear Daily* and *People* StyleWatch!) and I was even chosen as one of *Latina* magazine's "Latinas of the Year" in 2013. I still have to pinch myself sometimes to make sure it's all real.

But let's get something straight: *The Sweet Life* is a book about *you*. Sure, my name may be on it, and there's lots of personal stuff about me and the lessons I've learned over the course of my life within its pages, but I wrote this book to help *you* find happiness and success. My goal is not only to give you real-life tools for tackling the roadblocks you're bound to encounter on your journey but also to help you see that the strength you need to get through them in one piece has been inside you all along. And I'm here to help you tap into it.

So how do I plan on doing this? Well, by being totally, unabashedly honest about the mistakes that taught me valuable lessons, the failures that led to unforeseen opportunities, and, of course, the wins (both big and small) that gave me the motivation to keep at it. With each chapter we'll dive into some really juicy stuff, like the importance of knowing your self-worth, the magic that comes with discovering your passion, and the value in embracing fear. I'll also throw out suggestions for steps you can start taking toward success pretty much right away. Let's get started!

Chapter 1

My Not-So-Sweet Early Years

In the past few years, I have achieved success far beyond what I ever imagined was possible. I have a great career doing what I love most. I get to travel the world and meet the amazing people who watch my videos on YouTube. I have a beautiful house in a beautiful neighborhood that I share with my sweet husband, Jesse, and my son, Izek. I won't lie—it's a pretty great life. A *sweet* life, in fact. But that wasn't always the case.

If you've watched my channel, you know a little about my past—I was born in Mexico, immigrated to the United States with my family when I was little, grew up in California, served in the military, and then launched my YouTube channel to wild success. That's the gist of it, but it's far from the whole story.

In reality, nothing is that simple in life—especially not in mine. I've been blessed with so much—an amazing, tight-knit family being the most important—but there were a lot of disappointments and failures, too, and I could have easily ended up on a very different path. Ultimately, I'm going to spend most of this book sharing my secrets for success, and I hope my story inspires you to do what you love, challenge yourself, and reach your full potential. But before we launch into that, I want to share a bit about my beginnings, so if you're out there struggling, wondering if you'll ever have the opportunities you hope for, or thinking about giving up completely, you'll learn that no matter how dark things get, there is hope.

Coming to America

I was born in the summer of 1987 in Michoacán, a western state in Mexico where the majority of the population made their living in agriculture, fishing, or crafts. My father, Jaime Tejeda, was one of eight kids born to a poor family from a tiny rural town outside Michoacán. He never went to college but was able to get a respectable job as a banker, allowing him to support my mom, Maria Teresa, me, and my sisters, Cynthia Lizbeth and Ivette Paulina, in a modest yet comfortable and happy home.

One of my first memories as a kid is watching my dad

leave for the office in his tailored suit, his hair combed back, with a shiny leather briefcase in tow. To me, he looked important and strong, much like the superheroes from my morning cartoons. His careful approach to dressing and grooming was something I picked up on right away. Though we weren't rich by any means, his job was important and came with quite a bit of status, and he always made sure his immaculate appearance reflected that.

My mom would send my dad off with a peck on the cheek, then take her post in the kitchen to make her signature *chilaquiles* (lightly fried tortillas smothered in salsa verde) for me and my sisters. Then it was off to kindergarten for Cynthia and me while my mother took care of Ivette Paulina and managed the Tejeda household.

When Cynthia and I got home, we'd head straight to the backyard to play with our dogs and pet donkeys (yes, we had donkeys). Our mom continued her chores and took breaks to chase us around the yard as we played our favorite game, *escondidas*, a Mexican version of hide-and-seek. We'd spend entire afternoons in the sun running around without a care in the world, heading inside only when we heard our dad pull up to the house from work.

Dinnertime was sensory overload: the smell of homemade tortillas sizzling on the skillet, the kids shrieking over one another for a chance to spill the highlights of the day. Cynthia Lizbeth was the oldest and, naturally, also the loudest. But my dad always made sure I got a chance to fill him in on my day's important events ("Cynthia scraped her knee! I found a bird's nest!"). Ivette Paulina, who was just a toddler back then, would happily giggle along as the rest of us chatted.

Life was good. We weren't rich, but we were safe and taken care of and happy. Unbeknownst to us kids, however, our parents were making plans to leave it all behind.

I know what you're probably thinking: If life was so great for our family, why did my parents decide to leave Mexico? I have often wondered the same thing, and to be honest, I'll never really understand why we moved. According to my parents, in addition to wanting to get away from Mexico's not-so-great economic situation, immigrating to the US was simply the fashionable thing to do at the time. America was considered the land of opportunity, and the middle class was booming. There were endless possibilities for hard-working families looking for a higher standard of living. My parents had many family members and friends who had already made the move to the States. Their whispers of bigger and better opportunities were getting too loud to ignore. To me, America might as well have been a made-up place. I was so content with my life that the thought of living somewhere else never even crossed my mind, and my parents kept their plans to themselves during the two years they were planning the move.

When I was four years old, my dad traveled to Oxnard, California, to visit his brother Miguel, who had moved there nineteen years before and had found a job on a farm. My dad planned to visit for a month to use up his acquired time off at the bank, get a sense of the place, and then return to Mexico so he and my mom could start the lengthy immigration process. (Due to strict policies at the time, immigrating to America legally was virtually impossible without getting buried under mountains of paperwork and years of waiting.) To kill time and make a few bucks while Uncle Miguel was at work, my dad took a temporary job working on the same farm Uncle Miguel worked on.

And then something unexpected happened. He started to like working in the fields! Apparently, there had been rumors flying around his office that, due to the failing economy, the bank might go under, and my dad had realized his job was not as secure as he'd thought. Not only that, but he was making almost as much money on the farm as he had back home, with a lot more job security.

My father felt the opportunities for growth, financial stability, and success in the US were worth swapping his prestigious banking job for manual work. So rather than return home, he and my mom decided that it was best he stay in America and continue working on the farm until the rest of us could join him in California. My dad would continue to work on that farm for the next twenty-two years.

Meanwhile, my mother was left on her own to raise us in Mexico. As far as my sisters and I were concerned, it was business as usual. We were constantly reassured that we'd all be reunited very soon, though because we were so young, no one bothered to mention that the reunion would happen in America. To save money for the transition and allow my mom to take care of us full-time without having to worry about the bills, we moved in with our grandmother, our dad's mom, Mama Irene. My mom did such a good job of maintaining our daily routine—kindergarten, playtime, plenty of hugs and laughs—that other than missing our dad, my sisters and I were hardly aware that anything was different. We were still happy, no worries at all.

Now that I'm a mother myself, I can understand what a huge gamble my mom was taking. Keeping three little girls feeling secure while you're completely in the dark about what the future holds is no small feat. When asked about that time now, she shrugs and says that she did what she had to do for her family. I am still amazed at her strength and perseverance in the face of so much uncertainty.

As soon as my father felt stable, he arranged for us to meet him in the US. In the summer of 1994—two years after he left for America—he paid a pair of guides, or coyotes, that he found through acquaintances 3,000 pesos (about $220) to transport my mother, sisters, and me across the Mexico-US border. Though this was by no means legal, and coyotes were known to be a dangerous bunch, my parents had no choice but to trust them and hope for the best.

At six years old, you don't really question your parents when they tell you you're moving, but I do remember wondering why my mom was saying tearful good-byes to all her friends. Weren't we going to come back? I was confused, but as soon as I thought about seeing my dad again, all my questions and fears disappeared.

The first stop on our journey to California was a down-trodden motel on the Mexican side of the border a few hours away from Michoacán. The room was filthy and crawling with cockroaches. My mother refused to let us sit on the beds—not that any of us would want to. Our two guides were there waiting for us. A few hours before we planned to set out, they led us to the roof of the motel so we could get a preview of what lay ahead of us. From our perch, we watched as groups of other hopeful emigrants just like us jumped a fence and quickly scattered, only to be chased down by *la migra* (border patrol) in their huge black SUVs.

Watching all of this happen, I realized, for the first time, that I should be scared. My heart began to pound. My mom had done such a good job keeping the details of our move to herself, my sisters and I had no idea what to expect. The guides explained that the people going ahead of us were examples of what *not* to do. They told us to avoid *la migra*'s SUVs at all costs. Instead of running, we were supposed to hide behind rocks and bushes to keep from being spotted by the bright headlights as they swept across the landscape in search of movement. As far as instructions went, they couldn't be any clearer: Stay hidden and be quiet.

My mother, sisters, and I waited in that dingy motel room

until the clock struck two a.m. Go time. Our group scurried quietly to the fence. My mom went first, followed by the guides, who carried my sisters and me so we wouldn't fall behind. As I clung to the shoulders of my guide, I kept my eyes shut, thinking that if I couldn't see the immigration officers, they wouldn't be able to see me either.

I remember thinking how quickly we got to the other side. With us still tightly gripping their backs, the guides stayed low to the ground, crawling from rock to rock to avoid getting spotted by those headlights. Soon, curiosity overpowered fear, and I opened my eyes to watch the fence get smaller and smaller behind us.

We crawled for what felt like ages (in reality, the entire hike took no more than a few hours) until we came to a river called El Rio Grande (I later found out that a lot of people have drowned attempting the cross). Although I was tired and hungry, I knew complaining was out of the question. Ivette Paulina whimpered as we waded into the water, so I shot her a stern look. Thankfully, she seemed to understand my message to stay calm. Without even realizing exactly when it happened, we were out of the water and smack-dab in the middle of American suburbia. It was a different world compared to the one we'd left behind only a few hours ago. The simple stone houses and apartment buildings we knew were replaced by tract homes with lush green lawns and perfectly spaced streetlamps. We couldn't help but stop and stare until the guides reminded us to hurry along.

As our group weaved in and out of the streets and alleyways, making sure to stay hidden, our guides ran up driveways to pull at garage door handles in hopes of coaxing one open. My gut was telling me that sneaking around like this in the dark was bad and dangerous. I'd always relied on my mom to point out what's right and wrong, so whenever I started to feel anxious, I'd glance up to gauge her emotions, half expecting her to shoot me the stern look she'd usually give me when I misbehaved. But when we caught eyes, she gave me a quick smile and squeezed my hand. I took that as reassurance that even though this situation was far from normal, it was something we had to do.

After many attempts, a door finally slid up and in we went. That's how we spent our very first night in America: sleeping in the garage of a stranger who didn't even know we were there.

Once the sun came up, we left the garage and continued on foot to San Diego, where the guides said their curt good-byes and directed us to the airport. While my sisters and I were excited to see an airplane, my mom was desperately trying to keep her cool. This was the first time we were truly on our own, and we spoke virtually no English. To make sure we didn't do anything to arouse suspicion, my mom invented a "game" for us to play. The rules were simple: We had to pretend that we were Americans who had every right to be at that airport.

My mom bought each of us a can of Coke (which,

according to her, was what Americans drank), and we casually sipped our sodas as we walked through the airport. It worked. One of the guides had purchased our tickets earlier, and we got through security with zero complications, then quickly boarded the tiny commuter plane to Los Angeles.

As exhausted as my sisters and I were, we clambered over the armrests to look through the window at takeoff until we couldn't keep our eyes open anymore and dozed off. As we slept, my mom stayed on high alert. Even after we landed and proceeded to walk to the parking lot to meet my father and uncle, she didn't allow herself to relax. I could sense her tensing every time we passed a person in uniform. I'd never seen my happy, giggly mom act this way before: She saw everyone as a potential threat—from the TSA agent casually checking the line, to the flight attendants rushing to catch their flights—convinced they could all see right through us. If we were caught, we would've been sent right back to Mexico and the entire ordeal would've been for nothing.

My mother was barely thirty years old, not much older than I am right now, when she came to America with three kids in tow. Every time I think about her bravery, I'm overcome with gratitude and respect. Many years later my mother told me she was terrified of our guides the whole time we were in their care. Even before we set out on our journey, my mother was warned by others who'd crossed the border by way of coyotes that sexual assault was a very real threat for women making the trek alone. Because she was traveling with three young girls, the threat was even greater. Thankfully, my sisters and I were so young and naive that we didn't even understand such an awful scenario was possible, but for my mother, the fear for our innocence was very real.

When we walked out of the airport and saw my father waiting for us, my mother finally relaxed and leapt into his arms. It was jarring how tanned and weather-beaten my father looked. The crisp suit I expected to see him in had been replaced by dusty jeans, a flannel shirt, and work boots, but as far as I was concerned, his new look suited him just fine. He was still my dad, and we were finally a family again.

Home Sweet Home

Life in America was harder than it had been in Mexico, but in many ways it was the same. After a week or so of getting acclimated, my mother took a job on the same farm as my dad. My sisters and I started going to school right away. Picking up English was a breeze thanks to English as a Second Language classes. We spent our free time playing with the neighbor kids, running through the sprinklers over and over again until we were drenched.

Even though neither of my parents earned a lot of money, when it came time for dinner, we always had heaps of warm, delicious food on the table. And no matter how tired they were, my mom and dad would always ask us about what we learned at school and check in on whether we had done our homework. To save money, we rented a small trailer on the farm. Sure, things got a little snug—especially after my baby sister, Wendy Teresita, was born a year after our move—but my memories of that time are still fond. With so many people around, there wasn't an opportunity for any of us to feel lonely. Plus, our location provided tons of outdoor space where we could stretch our legs when things got a little crazy inside.

I realize now that, in spite of all the happy times we had together, my parents were struggling. For twenty-two years my father drove tractors around the fields to soften the dirt for crops, and my mother either gathered onions or worked the checkout aisle at Target, sometimes for as long as twelve hours a day. My parents had given up their middle-class life in Mexico so they could perform backbreaking labor in the hopes that their daughters would have the opportunity to do more—to go to college, have a career, earn enough to have a home and family and plenty of time to relax and enjoy life.

And as grateful as I was, and as much as I loved my parents, I came dangerously close to throwing all of that opportunity down the drain.

Bethany

I was a very happy kid, and when I was around my family and at home on the farm, I could be extremely outgoing and silly. Many of the photos from my childhood show me making a goofy face or giving one of my sisters bunny ears. But whenever I was around new people or in an unfamiliar environment, my spunkiness turned to shyness like *that*. I chalk it up to coming from a tight-knit family who knew me inside and out. I was comfortable around them, but strangers made me turn inward like a turtle retreating into its shell.

Because of this, I had a hard time making friends at school and was always envious of the kids, especially the girls, in my class who, I felt, were everything I wasn't—pretty, outgoing, popular, confident. At home, I felt unconditionally loved for who I was, but at school, I started comparing myself to other people. What they had—video games, CD players, the latest big-name sneakers—I didn't. (It didn't help that most of my clothes came secondhand from the Salvation Army since my parents couldn't afford to buy brand-new clothes for four rapidly growing girls.)

As a result, I did what so many girls do—I vied for the attention of the popular girls, the girls I wanted to be like, the girls who I desperately wanted to like me. There was one girl in particular, Bethany, who I looked up to as soon as I laid eyes on her. She was bubbly, and the teachers liked her, and for some reason, she took an interest in me. Unfortunately, Bethany turned out to be a fickle friend. You know the type: One moment she'd be saving a seat for me on the bus and whispering secrets into my ear, and the next she'd pretend she didn't even know who I was, or be angry at me for no reason. One time she even forced me to give her my prized sticker collection. If you are a child of the nineties, you know just how important stickers were, especially the Spice Girls ones. I had spent months collecting all of my favorites, and I loved being able to show them off to the other girls in class. Then one day Bethany told me she wouldn't be my friend anymore unless I gave her my beloved stickers. So I handed them over to her, and hid my face so she wouldn't see me cry.

Looking back now, I realize that Bethany probably suffered from her own feelings of inadequacy, no matter how perfect she appeared to be. She was a bully, someone who felt the need to put me down so she could feel better about herself. The only reason she pretended to be my friend was because she saw I was weak and knew she could take advantage. I don't want to imply that Bethany was some sort of sociopath—at some point, we've all treated someone badly who didn't deserve it. And I don't want to imply that Bethany is the reason I felt bad about myself. Eleanor Roosevelt once said, "No one can make you feel inferior without your consent." If I had felt good about myself, I would never have allowed Bethany, or anyone, to treat me that way. But because I was self-conscious and didn't feel like I was good enough, Bethany was able to hurt me all the more.

I'm not telling you this story because I think it's unique. I'll bet you've had a Bethany in your life at some point, too. If so, I hope you've cut her loose. If you still have a friend or acquaintance who makes you feel bad about yourself, I hope the lessons in this book will help you realize that you don't need her (or him).

Unfortunately for me, I didn't learn this lesson until much later. Bethany and I stayed "friends" through middle school. She continued to treat me horribly, and I continued to let her. At some point, we finally drifted apart. I wish I could say that I told her off and let it be known that I wouldn't tolerate her nastiness anymore. But it wasn't that dramatic, and unfortunately, even though Bethany was out of my life, my self-esteem was already damaged and high school didn't make it any easier.

Down Times in High School

Before she'd become a stay-at-home mom, and long before she took a job picking onions in a field all day, my mom had been your quintessential 1980s working girl. She'd been a secretary in a law firm, and her favorite part of the job was dressing up to go to the office. Every morning she'd don a power suit (complete with shoulder pads), do her hair and makeup, and head off to take on the day.

Even though she no longer had to dress up to go to work, she still believed young women should take care of their appearance. In middle school, I had started to develop an interest in makeup and beauty, but because my parents were strapped for cash, I didn't have the resources to let my budding interest fully bloom. But before my freshman year of high school, my mother started giving me an allowance—$20 every few weeks to spend on anything I wanted—which meant I finally had the means to put more thought and resources into the way I looked. I couldn't wait to leave dowdy junior high Dulce behind and start high school in style.

During my first ever solo shopping trip, I bought baby-blue pants—to go with a baby-blue shirt, of course—and a tin of matching eye shadow. And let me tell you, I was hot stuff. Well . . . at least I *thought* I was hot stuff.

In any case, the extra effort started to pay off. All of a sudden, my friends' brothers started chatting me up when I was at their house and older boys in high school started to take notice of me. The attention was actually beginning to make me feel better about myself! But here's the thing about relying on others to build up your confidence: It makes for a very fragile foundation upon which to build your self-worth—a lesson I learned the hard way when I experienced my first heartbreak.

It all started casually enough that same summer before

high school when a friend passed my phone number to Peter, her cute cousin who attended school a few towns over. Up until this point, my experience with boys was limited to awkward flirting and the occasional crush—nothing to call home about. But according to my friend, Peter was first-boyfriend material. Though we'd never met in person, I knew from the pictures in his junior high yearbook that he had adorable dimples, played basketball, and had a ton of friends. On paper, he was everything I could possibly want in a boyfriend.

The first time he called me couldn't have gone any better, and over the next few weeks, we spent hours talking about our Mexican upbringings and cracking each other up with silly jokes. I couldn't believe my luck! I had just turned fourteen and already met (well, sort of met) a great guy with whom I could really see a future. He told me that he'd never liked talking to a girl this much, that he loved my laugh, and that he couldn't wait to meet me. Before either of us had the chance to bring up an in-person first date, we found out that we were enrolled in the same summer school program. We were both thrilled at the prospect of finally meeting and attending the same school, even if it was just for a month. I spent the night before the first day of summer school planning my look (my baby-blue pants, a cute tank top, and LOTS of lip gloss), nervously imagining our first date and maybe even our first kiss. I was so excited, I couldn't fall asleep.

We arranged to meet outside after we were both done with our classes. I still hadn't left my grade school shyness behind, so I was nervous but kept telling myself this was different. Thanks to hours of phone conversations, Peter already knew me. And not only that, he liked me!

But the second Peter and I met in person, I registered a look of disappointment on his adorable face. I was praying that maybe I'd imagined it—maybe he was just as nervous as I was, which would explain why he wasn't making eye contact. But instead of the romantic scene I'd been imagining, what I got was cold, hard rejection. After a few minutes of awkward conversation—nothing like our marathon late-night chats—he mumbled something about needing to focus on basketball season and not having time for a girlfriend before quickly walking away. I was left standing there alone, in the middle of the school yard, on the verge of tears.

So there it was: all the proof I needed that I wasn't pretty enough to have a boyfriend. What other explanation could there possibly be? In all the time we'd spoken on the phone, Peter seemed genuinely interested in me, even excited about the prospect of dating me, so I knew it wasn't my personality that had turned him off. It was only after he laid eyes on me that he turned and ran. I spent the hour-long bus ride home sobbing uncontrollably; the only thought running through my mind was that I just wanted to disappear. I felt embarrassed and utterly alone, but worst of all, I felt unwanted.

My mom was in the kitchen when I got home. I didn't want to explain my tear-streaked, puffy face, so I bolted to my bedroom and locked the door. I had no idea what to do with myself. I'd seen movies and TV shows where characters who were emotionally distraught would take pills to stop the pain. The only pills I could find were a dozen Tylenol, so I swallowed them all.

I'm not sure what I expected to happen, but the pills didn't make me feel any better. They did, however, turn into a coping mechanism: Whenever I felt ugly, desperate, or low, I would console myself with a handful of pills. It was my little secret, my personal escape from the pain. Although taking too much Tylenol is super dangerous and has been shown to cause liver damage, I was lucky enough to escape the ill effects. But I did come to rely on the sense of control the pills offered to get me through the next four years. I couldn't control what others thought of me, and I certainly couldn't make myself into a different person. Taking the pills was the only thing I knew I could do to give myself a feeling of control.

The Downward Spiral

Before we dig into what happened next, I'd like to take a moment and tell you that sharing the details of this dark time in my life isn't easy for me. I debated for a long time whether I wanted to be 100 percent open about my state of mind and my actions. A big part of me is ashamed of how I handled myself back then, while another part of me can't help but wonder how different those years might have been had I gotten the professional help I clearly needed. In the end, I decided to share my story because I hope that the next few paragraphs might serve as a cautionary tale to anyone who has gotten so wrapped up in fitting in or being liked by others that she has forgotten what it's like to love herself. As uncomfortable and painful as my high school years were, I consider myself incredibly lucky to have left that part of my life behind and, most importantly, to have learned from it. But there are many who keep living with the pain. If you feel depressed, anxious, or suicidal, talk to someone. I wish I had. Don't let the pain eat away at you before it's too late. The truth is, when you're a teenager, life seems extra dramatic, and I promise you, it does get better! A lot of us go through growing pains at this age. Keeping those emotions to yourself only makes things worse. In my darkest times, when I couldn't express what I was feeling to anyone else, I'd spill my feelings in a journal. It wasn't a permanent solution, but I did get a sense of relief after writing out my trouble, even if it didn't last very long. It's okay to have these extreme feelings; just make sure you don't suppress them.

Because I was hurting from Peter's rejection, high school was off to a rocky start before it even began. For the next four years, I continued the negative pattern I'd started in grade school by keeping the pain to myself and taking pills when it got to be too much. I did manage to make a few good friends, but I never became that close with them because I was afraid to be vulnerable. The last time I'd put myself out there, thinking someone really liked me, he'd walked away the second he saw me. I couldn't bear to face that again.

Nowadays, people often tell me that I embody the American Dream—a daughter of immigrants whose sacrifice and hard work allowed her to achieve amazing success doing what she loves most. But in high school, I did pretty much everything I could to squander that opportunity. I didn't want to—I knew how much my parents wished for me to be a success and to live up to my potential, and I hated the idea of disappointing them—but in my desperate bid for attention, I went off the rails.

More than anything, I wanted to be like the popular kids. They always hung out together, went to parties, and wore the trendiest clothes I'd lust over in *Teen* and *Seventeen* magazines. But even with my allowance, I didn't have the money to dress like them, so in an effort to fit in somewhere, I fell in with the wrong crowd. I started cutting class, not turning in homework assignments, and mouthing off to teachers. Let's just say high school Dulce was not very sweet. To make the cool kids notice me, I'd ditch school, drink alcohol, and stay out way too late. I knew my actions would disappoint my parents, but I was so obsessed with being liked that I let it take control of me. I worked so hard to please people who didn't care about me at the expense of my parents' feelings. I wish I'd figured that out sooner.

I also started dating the guy version of Bethany, a boy named Michael I met at the beginning of freshman year and continued seeing on and off for the next four years. I was so thrilled to meet a guy who could take my mind off of Peter's rejection that I was willing to put up with Michael's bad-boy ways. He was constantly in and out of juvenile detention for fighting, drugs, and violating probation. He also (surprise, surprise) cheated on me on a regular basis. But I felt like Michael was the best I could do. I even began to think that his constant cheating was my fault. Maybe if I figured out a way to make him happy, he wouldn't feel the need to do it anymore. So I took him back every single time he hurt me in the hopes that he'd change. He didn't.

All my acting out did end up gaining me some attention, but not the kind I wanted. One day, while making my second-period escape from school, a boy I'd known since ninth grade walked by and muttered, "You're just a lowlife, aren't you?" Those words hit me harder than a punch in the gut. Not only did my classmates not think I was cool, they thought I was a loser. And the worst part was, I thought I was a loser, too. I wasn't proud of myself. I didn't like being the bad kid in class or failing every subject. Every fiber of my being wanted to shout, "I do care! I want to be good!

Don't you see this is all a charade?" But of course, I just kept on walking. I didn't know what else to do.

These constant feelings of unworthiness and the negative state of mind I was in sparked a vicious cycle—I felt guilty about all the bad things I did, for letting my parents down and not trying hard in school, and so I punished myself. I scratched my skin until it bled and swallowed pills to try and numb the pain and fool myself into thinking that I had some form of control over my life.

My parents could tell something was wrong, but because I kept the details and the self-harm hidden, they didn't know the extent of it. Hispanic families are generally insular—problems are kept under wraps and solved within the confines of the home. They felt my behavior was their responsibility. And in any case, they probably didn't realize that my problems were not only greater than I let on but also out of their control. What I really needed was professional help, which I know my parents would have provided had they known I was hurting myself. Both my mom and my dad did everything they could to get me to come to my senses. My mom spent hours sitting by my bedside while I wept, stroking my hair and pleading with me to tell her why I was acting out. Sometimes, the conversation turned heated. Once she caught me sneaking out to meet Michael, and she said something I hope to never have to say to my child: "No boy who only wants to see you at two a.m. will ever respect you." Unfortunately, I didn't understand the wisdom in those words, only how much they hurt, and I kept seeing Michael. My dad was more of a disciplinarian, setting a curfew and cutting off my allowance. But that just made me act out more.

I somehow managed to graduate high school, but much to my parents' disappointment, my lackluster grades put college out of reach. I took a job manning the register at Hobby People (a store best known for selling model airplanes) for minimum wage and continued to see Michael. Finally, when he cheated on me yet again, I got fed up and broke it off for good. With Michael out of the picture, I felt ready to do something dramatic, something that would get me out of this rut and take my life in a new direction.

A few months before graduation, an army recruiter had come to speak to my class about all the opportunities the army could afford—a great career, a chance to go to college, travel opportunities, and the honor of serving your country. I was hardly combat ready, but all that sounded better than ringing up crafting supplies for eight hours a day. I found his card and dialed the number for the Oxnard army recruitment center.

A man's voice answered. He wasn't particularly kind or caring, and yet I couldn't stop myself from spilling my heart out to him. I told this complete stranger how sick I was of my life, how desperate and hopeless I felt, how I just needed to start over. He told me the army was the place to do it and to come into the recruitment center first thing Monday morning.

I wanted to leave my life behind as fast as possible, and within a week, I had quit my job and informed my parents of my decision to enlist in the army. Understandably, my parents were stunned, but they understood why I felt the need to do something drastic. I was determined to make them proud. So I packed a bag, boarded a bus, and headed off to the next chapter of my life.

Chapter 2

From Boot Camp to Beauty Guru: How the Army Transformed My Life and Led Me to Discover My Passion

My military career began in January of 2006, when I started basic training, and continued until May 2009, when I decided to leave the army behind. A lot of people are shocked to discover that I served in the army—including a fifteen-month tour in Iraq—purely because of how I look (I'm four foot nine and quite petite) and the fact that I love fashion and beauty. I credit my time in the army with helping me grow up. I can say with full confidence that if I hadn't made that call to the Oxnard recruiting office, you would not be reading this book, and I would not be as successful as I am today.

Two things happened during my service that helped transform the shy, insecure, troubled girl that I was into the woman I am today. The first was that I learned that I am capable of far more than I had thought possible—both physically and emotionally. The second was that I cultivated my passion—a lifelong love of fashion and beauty—into a successful career.

The story of how that happened is not only entertaining (I hope); it's also proof that opportunity can be found in the most unexpected places and that all of your life experiences—from the dramatic to the mundane—shape who you are.

The Basic Rules of Basic Training

From the moment our bus from the airport pulled into South Carolina's Fort Jackson, I knew I was in for a wild ride. For the most part, the other soldiers and I remained silent, anticipating what would be waiting for us. Naively, I believed that it wouldn't be as bad as the movies made it out to be. The people I had met during onboarding (the army's registration process) were nothing but gracious and kind, leading me to believe that basic training would be the same.

When we got off the bus, we were greeted by a bunch of drill sergeants screaming curse words and incomprehensible commands in our faces. I stood there with my mouth gaping while a blur of loud voices and strange faces whirled around me. My mind went totally blank, and all I felt was a type of fear I hadn't felt in a long, long time. The fear of the unknown. Though I was really afraid, the profanities the drill sergeants were screaming weren't as bad as the terrible things I'd been telling myself for years.

These drill sergeants were tasked with making sure we left basic training as the most disciplined versions of ourselves. Essentially, they break you down and strip you of everything you were before the army so they can build you right back up to be the best soldier you can be. To outsiders, it may seem like intimidation and abuse, but all the yelling and trash talk is designed to prepare you for the grueling nature of combat. If you can't keep your cool while someone is screaming obscenities in your face, how are you supposed to function when enemies are shooting at you? Starting day one, the army imposes as many rules as possible on our behavior. We were told where to look (eyes straight when your drill sergeant is speaking to you), what to drink (two gallons of water, every day, without exception), and who we could go to the bathroom with (your battle buddy, a preassigned partner that you have to travel everywhere with).

You'd think, with my track record, I would have had a hard time following these rules. But as crazy as it sounds, I was happy someone else was finally taking control of my out-of-control life. For so long I had tried, in vain, to rein myself in, but the only control I was able to assert in my life was by hurting myself. It was my only hope of getting a second chance. I had spent so many years breaking the rules that for once I just wanted to follow them. And not only that, I wanted to *master* them. I was so desperate and in need of direction that I willingly handed over my time, my body, and my mind into the army's care. I knew, somehow, that if I did, things would finally change.

And I was right. It wasn't easy, and I'll admit that in the beginning, I often felt like giving up when faced with a physical challenge I wasn't prepared for. But soon I made a commitment to myself: I didn't have to be able to do everything perfectly the second I was told to—I just had to force myself to try. When I started basic training, I couldn't do a push-up or run a mile, so I wasn't surprised when I didn't become fit overnight. It helped that I had drill sergeants yelling at me all day, but slowly I found that if I put my mind to something and worked really hard, I could get better.

As my body grew stronger, so did my mind. My body was doing incredible things, and I felt thankful for my legs, arms, and overall strength for the first time in years. I felt whole and worthwhile. Not only did I no longer need to take pills to feel in control, I actually felt like I had something to offer the world. I never wanted to lose that feeling.

After thirteen grueling weeks of physical training, I got the opportunity to show what I was really made of. For our final test our entire company spent ten days in the wilderness. All 120 of us, both men and women, had to march in formation for twelve miles to get to our new camp. This

long distance is difficult even for those in peak physical con-
dition, but marching in formation while carrying a seventy-
pound rucksack is a whole 'nother monster. What "marching
in formation" means is that all of us had to keep up the same
pace. I am four foot nine, so I knew I was going to have a
hard time staying in line surrounded by a bunch of six-foot-
plus men. I was somewhere in the middle of the pack, and as
far as my eyes could see, I was surrounded by camouflaged
chests—the midsections of the men and women whose long
strides meant I had to march double time.

At this point, I was in the best shape of my life. I could do
over fifty push-ups and sit-ups without breaking a sweat. I
could run a mile in under seven minutes. I could even do upward of twenty pull-ups. I had calluses on my palms and was
beginning to see the beginnings of a six-pack on my once
soft stomach. I had joined the army to prove there was more
to me than just a series of failures. I wanted to prove it to my
parents, to the popular kids back home, to the teachers whose
classes I had flunked, and to every boy who had hurt me. But
most of all, I needed to prove it to myself—and for the first
time in my life, I believed I could.

Before we set out on our trek, I knew that I wanted to test
myself. I needed to see what I was capable of, both mentally
and physically. So I set a seemingly simple goal: I would not
allow myself to fall out of line. As the miles trudged on, more
and more people fell out—they were hot and they were tired.
And though I couldn't blame them, I refused to be one of

them. "Left, right, left, right," I kept thinking to myself. My inner voice was my own personal drill sergeant: "I *will not* fall out of line."

By mile seven the sweat was pouring down my face and the salt stung my eyes. I was short of breath, and my body was screaming that it couldn't keep going. I gritted my teeth and kept my eyes on the prize. I just kept repeating to myself, to the beat of our march, left, right, left, right: "I will not fall out, I will not fall out, I will not fall out." Finally, after we finished our last excruciating mile, the entire company collapsed on the dusty field of our campsite, chests heaving and gulping in as much air as possible despite the heavy South Carolina heat. I had made it. I had done one of the most challenging things I'd ever had to do, and I'd made it! I'd been marching next to a soldier named Tang the entire twelve miles, and after our breathing slowed and we finally started feeling normal again, he pulled me aside. "Dang, Tejeda," he said, "you did good. You didn't fall out of line, not even once." It was the best compliment anyone had ever given me, and even as the soreness set in, I was on cloud nine. It was official. I was a changed person.

To this day, I still carry a lot of the lessons of basic training with me. For one, I realize the magic of discipline, of pushing yourself to the next level even if it's uncomfortable, of never giving up, of believing you can do something if you put your mind to it. It may sound like clichéd advice, but I know from experience that it's easier said than done.

Even if you've never had a drill sergeant scream orders in your face, or even if you've never had to follow rules telling you how to go to the bathroom or when to eat, you can apply discipline to your own life. Ever made a plan to go to the gym, only to decide you're too tired and stay in and watch TV instead? How did that make you feel? Probably lazy and disappointed in yourself. On the other hand, when you actually get off your tush, trudge to the gym, and sweat for a bit, even though you'd rather be somewhere else, how great do you feel when you're finished? When you make a commitment—whether it's to yourself or someone else—and follow through, amazing things happen.

Finding Beauty in Basic Training

One of the ways the military enforces discipline and transforms cadets from civilians into soldiers is by forcing them to conform, to do without the things they think they "need." So, when I showed up on day one of basic training, I was handed greenish-brown, oversize fatigues, and told I couldn't wear an ounce of makeup. I wasn't thrilled about this. Since I was thirteen years old, I'd relied on makeup and fashion—heavily done-up eyes, super glossy lips, tight jeans, and revealing tops—to mask what I really felt inside: insecure, unworthy, and most definitely not beautiful. Makeup was my armor, the only thing separating me from even more rejection and pain.

A lot of people approach makeup this way. We use it to cover up our perceived flaws or change something we don't like about ourselves. Or we use it to make ourselves look the way we think we're supposed to look, copying the latest trends from magazines, never pausing to consider whether or not we truly like what we see in the mirror. I was certainly guilty of this, so the prospect of spending my days surrounded by strangers, without an ounce of makeup to protect me, was scary. But then a funny thing happened. I became so focused on my basic needs—passing fitness tests, drinking gallons of water, learning the importance of teamwork—that I actually *forgot* to worry about how I looked. Things like mascara and the latest trends proved to be completely insignificant when all my energy went toward building up stamina and survival skills. It helped that everyone around me looked exactly the same and I didn't have access to TV or magazines—there weren't any opportunities to compare my outfit or hairstyle to someone else's, a freedom I had never felt in the civilian world.

It's an interesting experiment: Put hundreds of people together and strip them of the external things they believe are the sum of their identities. Rather than hide behind makeup, jewelry, or brand-name clothes and shoes, we were one homogenous group in camouflage. We were equals, no longer defined by our material possessions, and forced to tackle the same challenges as everyone around us. This not only helped me feel better about myself; it also helped me connect with my fellow soldiers. For the first time in my life, I didn't feel judged based on my looks—what made me stand out to my fellow soldiers was my character and accomplishments.

My relationship with my body also changed dramatically. Before joining the army, I was never particularly fit or active. In fact, because I was so depressed, I had very little energy to motivate myself to do much of anything. But with intense daily exercise, proper nutrition, and plenty of new-found motivation, I could lug around rucksacks that weighed almost as much as I did, and run for miles at a time. I treated my body well, and in turn, my body gave me strength I never knew I had. Instead of letting makeup and clothes define who I was or how I felt about myself, I began appreciating my body for its strength and myself as a whole for having the perseverance to power through.

Making Up with Makeup

Though I no longer *needed* makeup to make me feel whole, I still *missed* it the way a ballerina might miss the barre or a painter her watercolors. All of a sudden, makeup became a means of self-expression, a creative outlet, and I couldn't wait to get my paws on some. Luckily, one of the privileges of completing basic training for female soldiers is looser makeup regulations. So by the time I arrived in Iraq in September

2006—after thirteen weeks of Military Occupational Specialty (MOS) training, during which I learned to do the job the army had assigned me: fixing generators!—I was allowed to wear mascara and lip gloss during work hours and even get my nails done. On weekends, all bets were off.

But rather than get all dolled up to impress someone, I would have a blast experimenting with different products and practicing the glam looks I saw in magazines. While other cadets ordered PlayStations, video games, and DVDs, I wanted nothing more than to build up my makeup collection. Even though I didn't have access to huge department stores or beauty supply outlets (I would dream about Sephora and kept a massive mental shopping list of things I'd treat myself to when I got out), my army salary still allowed me to do a fair amount of online shopping. And because army bases are still considered US territory, shipping charges were surprisingly affordable.

Rather than spend a ton on one really expensive eye shadow palette, I liked stocking up on several cheaper options so I could try as many shades as possible. I know many women have their trusted brands, colors, and specific looks that work for them, but not me! I loved testing all sorts of different products—and still do.

I would order just about every blush, shadow, and lipstick from the e.l.f. line, because they were inexpensive and came in a rainbow of colors, and eagerly wait the two weeks for my shipment to arrive. The freedom to have makeup again was special to me on several levels. In a way, I was experiencing it for the first time. Doing my makeup wasn't a necessity anymore; it was a source of pure joy.

There was only one thing I treasured more than my modest makeup assortment . . . my MASSIVE magazine collection. The tiny Post Exchange store on base carried a selection of fashion and lifestyle magazines, and each month I would pick up issues of *Cosmopolitan*, *Allure*, and *Teen Vogue*, and spend every minute of downtime reading each one cover to cover. As I read, I would tear out pages with outfits I admired, beautiful editorials, and motivational quotes and plaster them all over the walls of my bunk. Studying those magazines was the only way I could educate myself about an industry to which I felt so deeply connected.

At this point, the thought of fashion or beauty as a career hadn't even crossed my mind—I saw it as a hobby, an escape after a long day of physical and mental labor. I treasured those magazines like some people treasure their favorite books or photos, and by the time I returned to the United States, I'd saved an entire boxful—which I shipped home with me. Because we were each allowed no more than two boxes of personal belongings to ship back, my fellow soldiers made fun of me for wasting precious cargo space on what they considered useless junk, but the magazines were so much more to me than out-of-date glossies; they were a portal into a world I so desperately coveted.

I had no way of knowing this at the time, but all of that

practicing in Iraq was laying the groundwork for what would become my life's calling. As I said, I never thought my love for makeup could translate into a career, but even in the middle of Iraq I was gaining a reputation for being a fashionista. And while plenty of people didn't take me seriously (some even made fun of me) for my interest in what they saw as a frivolous activity, others recognized my passion for what it was—a key part of who I am.

One of those people was Sergeant Lockett, a tall, handsome, and very intelligent man in his fifties. I always had a soft spot for Sergeant Lockett because, while he was definitely tough and demanded respect, he never barked out orders or treated us like dogs. He saw each one of us as individuals, not cogs in a wheel or subordinates to be kept in line, and he actively encouraged us to embrace our individuality. He would even tell us stories about his own personal life, making him more human in our eyes. I learned that he spoke fluent Italian because he had been stationed in Tirrenia, Italy, for a long time. Once, while we were working together on the same convoy team, he even told me the story of how he met his Italian wife there. I loved hearing this seemingly intimidating man gush about the love of his life. I was his subordinate, but I always felt as if he respected me and appreciated me for who I was.

My first Christmas in Iraq, our platoon did a Secret Santa gift exchange and Sergeant Lockett handed me a present. It was a sketchbook with instructions on how to draw fashion figures. I actually teared up. It was the absolute last thing I expected—especially from a tough-guy army sergeant. I was so touched and, honestly, a little bit amazed that I was being recognized for something positive, not to mention something I loved! It's still the best gift I've ever received.

From that point on, the book and I were inseparable—if I wasn't fulfilling one of my work duties, at the gym, or spending time with Jesse (my boyfriend, now husband, whom I met while in Iraq . . . more on him later), I was in my bunk teaching myself to sketch. It's during those happy moments with my sketchbook that I started thinking about fashion as a career possibility.

Saying Good-Bye to the Army

By March 2008 I was back from Iraq and stationed at Fort Hood—a massive base in Texas—waiting for the last nine months of my active duty term to expire. When you join the military, you are obligated to serve eight years, but you do have the option to pick how many of those years are active duty. I chose three years and signed up to serve in the reserves till 2011. This meant that I could be called back to deploy at any given time and had to dedicate one weekend a month and two weeks out of the year to attending field training exercises. It was during my time in the reserves that

I became a sergeant, which is a well-respected rank that's hard to achieve and comes with a lot of responsibility.

I knew that reenlisting as active duty wasn't in my future. Although it was the most transformative experience of my life, I didn't want to make the military my career. The army had served its purpose at a time in my life when I needed its rules. But I was not cut out for battle or deployment; plus, I'd reached a point where I was growing tired of the constant micromanaging.

As much as I was itching to move on with my life, I wasn't blind to the fact that my time in the military had given me something I'd never had before: options. That was a pretty huge deal for someone like me, who, up until the day I joined the army, didn't really have any options, much less any hope for a future. Not only was I equipped with an amazing set of marketable skills (strong work ethic, great leadership and communication skills) that looked impressive on a résumé, thanks to the GI Bill, which provides all sorts of benefits for vets, including tuition payment, I could actually afford a college education.

As I waited out my last few months of active duty, I contemplated my next move. I could go to trade school (I was seriously considering becoming a dental assistant), apply to fashion school (I'd started following Lauren Conrad in Iraq and had become interested in attending the Fashion Institute of Design and Merchandising in Los Angeles, just like her), or continue doing what I was trained for in the army and find a job fixing generators (most definitely the easiest choice of the bunch).

My parents and Jesse promised to be 100 percent supportive of whatever decision I made. Knowing that they were confident I'd make the right choice made the process easier. Plus, I knew, whatever choice I made, I'd have the skills I learned in the military to help me follow through. Despite all of this pondering, I fell into my eventual career gradually and by accident. In fact, it actually started with a failure.

Chapter 3

Progress, Not Perfection: Keep Moving Forward and Figure Out the Details Later

I wish I could say that after I left Iraq, I came home and decided to dedicate myself full throttle to pursuing a beauty career. The truth is, as much as the army had helped me take control of my life and set me on the right path, I was still listless. I was torn between taking a chance on what I loved—fashion and beauty—and sticking with a more "obvious" career—one that was secure and safe and relatively easy to start in.

My self-esteem had been transformed, but I still wasn't confident that I could make it in the fashion world. It was competitive, I had zero experience, and as much as I imagined what life would be like working as a designer or a consultant for a major brand, it still felt very much out of my reach.

It was during this phase of my life that I initially launched my YouTube channel, Dulce Candy. When I did it, I had no way of knowing what it would grow into or that it would lead to all the opportunities I've had since then—partnerships with major brands, interviews and profiles in my favorite magazines, guest appearances on shows like *Project Runway* and *Good Morning America* and events like the Teen Choice Awards.

When I think back to that time and rewatch some of those earlier videos, I can see just how far I've come. I like to reflect on each of the steps that got me to where I am today. Some were definitely bigger than others, and I've made plenty of mistakes along the way, too, but I've learned from all of them and realized that everything in life is just a series of steps. It's okay if you don't have your future figured out just yet. Or, if you know what you want to do and have your eye on the prize but find that you're not getting there as quickly as you want, that's okay, too.

Even now, I sometimes get down on myself if I make a mistake, if a video doesn't get as many views as I think it should, or if I trip over my words in an interview. But there's a phrase I've adopted that makes me feel better: "Progress, not perfection." Success doesn't happen overnight. Rome wasn't built in a day. If you want to do something BIG, you have to get over a lot of small hurdles first. When you start to feel discouraged, just remember that every experience you have helps you grow, helps you learn, helps you become better. Embracing this will help you lead the sweet life you've always wanted.

Don't Sell Yourself Short (Sales Is *Not* for Everyone)

Three months into my active duty, I went back home to Oxnard to visit my family for two weeks of R & R. I was still trying to figure out what my next step would be after my military service ended, and in an effort to learn more about different options, I asked Cynthia if I could go with her to one of her Mary Kay meetings. Cynthia had been a Mary Kay salesperson for four years. She'd started when she was eighteen and had become one of the top consultants in her market. As the eldest of our sisters, Cynthia had always been the most driven and serious, and I'd always admired her for taking control of her life at such a young age. I figured, even if I didn't end up following in my sister's footsteps, at least it was a step toward determining what to do with my future

The way Mary Kay works is that every woman is considered her own boss with her own business. The consultants (as they're called) order makeup and skin care products at discounted prices and then sell them to their clients for a profit. At their meetings, the consultants discuss successful selling approaches and business-building strategies so I figured I might just learn a thing or two—and maybe even launch my own Mary Kay business. On the face of it, it seemed like the perfect fit—I could make money working with makeup! How awesome is that?

When Cynthia and I got to the meeting, I was instantly embraced by the other sales reps. The atmosphere in the room was all about support and inspiration. There was no cattiness, no competition, no put-downs. Just a group of smart, successful women sharing their experiences and advice on entrepreneurship. No wonder Cynthia was hooked. Save for Sergeant Lockett and a few friends, the rest of the people I'd met in the army couldn't have cared less about my interest in beauty and fashion. At Mary Kay, it wasn't just encouraged and accepted; it was a job requirement!

It seemed like I had finally found a way to make my love for makeup into a career, and I wasn't about to let my lack of sales experience get in the way. As soon as I got back to Texas I spent about $600 (an obscene amount for anyone, especially me at the time) on a starter kit. The kit was full of testers, brushes, applicators, mirrors, and order forms—which, in addition to actual products, were necessary to use at Mary Kay parties. These gatherings were supposed to bring together a bunch of like-minded women—friends, family, and acquaintances—under the guise of a party with drinks and desserts, but really, they were meant to be opportunities for me to sell products. Once I sold out of my initial stock, I'd be able to order more based on what my customers wanted.

While I was waiting for my products to arrive, I started attending the weekly Wednesday night meetings in Killeen. To find more women to invite to parties, one of the techniques consultants used was to approach strangers directly, start an innocent conversation by paying them some sort of compliment not based on their appearance, and then launch into a Mary Kay pitch. Ideally, this pitch would intrigue the woman and make her want to learn more about the product, which would be the perfect opportunity to invite her to a party.

The thought of approaching strangers and chatting them up completely terrified me. My confidence might have improved, but I still felt shy around new people, and up until that point, my only sales experience was working at Hobby People, which hardly counted. But thanks to my training sessions, I developed a plan: Drive into a gas station, chat up every woman I saw, then give her my business details or invite her to a Mary Kay party.

It seemed simple. How hard could it be to chat someone up about makeup—the thing I love talking about pretty much more than anything? So after attending our meeting and neatly organizing my kit, I got in my car at 5:30 p.m. and drove to a gas station next to an office building with the hope of catching women on their way home from work.

When it came down to it, I couldn't even get out of my

car. Every time I saw a potential client pull in, I tried to psych myself up by repeating all the positive affirmations I'd picked up at the training sessions ("When you come to a roadblock, take a detour," "People fall forward to success"). Instead of the successful scenarios described in those meetings, all I could picture was rejection. I decided to cut my losses and go home.

I ended up making a few more attempts at kick-starting my business. I even printed out flyers with the intention of putting them up in my neighborhood but chickened out. How could I be a successful saleswoman if the thought of posting flyers was too much to bear? I went to a few more meetings, but I'd already decided I didn't have it in me to be a salesperson.

That's not to say that had I practiced and forced myself to climb out of my shell I wouldn't have gotten good at selling. But I knew in my heart that I wasn't meant to be a salesperson. Mary Kay sounded great in theory, but the truth is, really good salespeople are naturally charming, articulate, confident people—and those were not my strengths. There was no way trying to sell makeup to women for profit would make me happy, so I decided to move on to the next thing, even if I didn't know what that thing was. But that's the beauty of opportunity: It can take on many forms. It can even hide in plain sight as failure. In my case, failing at sales was a true blessing—or should I say opportunity—in disguise.

Flip Failure into Fortune

Adding insult to injury, I had $600 worth of products taking up space in my hallway. It might have been obvious that I sucked at selling, but there was no way I was going to let perfectly good makeup go to waste.

This was the summer of 2008. YouTube was still in its infancy but was already gaining huge traction online. At the time, people mostly used it to watch random videos, and the biggest "celebrities" were people who posted one-off funny videos that went viral. It wasn't a place where people went to make money or launch a brand, but beauty tutorials had already started catching on. It was the perfect medium—unlike a magazine, you could actually watch real people doing their makeup and hair, and it was so easy to find what you were looking for. If you wanted to learn how to apply liquid eyeliner, you just had to search in one place and a bunch of homemade videos would appear.

I'd used YouTube a few times to pick up pointers, and I loved how natural and conversational the people in the videos were. Most of these videos were made by regular girls just like me, who loved makeup and wanted nothing more than to share their tips and tricks with the world. There was no fancy editing or camerawork or designed sets, so you connected to the people in the videos. They weren't trying to make money or sell you something, and they didn't work for anyone but themselves so they could just be who they were. After attempting to act like someone I wasn't by selling makeup products to strangers in a gas station, I found that very appealing.

For months I had thought about posting my own video, and this finally felt like the right time to try. I signed up for a YouTube account and published my first video: a shaky, out-of-focus smoky eye shadow tutorial using some of my leftover Mary Kay products, which I shot using an old point-and-shoot camera. I spent the entire three minutes and forty-three seconds stuttering through the tutorial . . . without actually demonstrating any of the steps. It was a disaster.

Not only did the video bomb, but the comments people left were brutal: My voice was trembling, I was mumbling, and I barely looked at the camera. I took the video down almost immediately. The old me would have chalked the experience up to just another failure and left it at that. But I wasn't about to give up. I loved talking about makeup, especially after a day drowning in car parts at the motor pool. Even though the video wasn't exactly great, I had really enjoyed making it! After getting down and dirty in the motor pool nine hours a day, the thought of heading straight to the shower and glamming myself up to film a video sounded pretty great. It was downright therapeutic.

So the very next day, I went back to YouTube and studied other videos I liked. I used the comments I'd received as constructive criticism. My second video—another eye shadow tutorial, called "Mary Kay, The Berries Look!"—was much better than the first one. The video quality still wasn't perfect, and there was little editing to speak of, but I made sure to sound more confident, to keep my tone casual yet authoritative, and to look directly at the camera as if I was making eye contact with my viewers.

To my great surprise, the responses—all twelve of them—were much more positive the second time around. People liked my conversational tone and seemed to find my tips genuinely helpful! From that point on, I continued making videos pretty much daily for the next seven years and loving every second of it. In the beginning, I didn't think my YouTube channel would be anything more than a hobby, but the better I got at it, the more I started to see it for what it really was—an expression of my passion. As of this writing, I've made close to eight hundred videos—go back to the very beginning and check out some of my earlier tutorials. You'll see how far I've come, and get a good laugh in the process. Shooting, editing, and publishing each and every one of those videos has taught me something new about my business and motivated me to keep striving to get better at what I do.

You'll Never Get to Where You're Going If You're Lost on Someone Else's Path

Even after my channel started gaining momentum, I couldn't help but feel that the pace I was going wasn't quite fast enough. Vloggers who had started their channels around the same time I did were outperforming me. I would get discouraged and, I'm embarrassed to say, more than a little bit jealous. I'd watch them get the massive brand contracts, huge advertising deals, even coveted TV appearances, and get totally hung up on why it wasn't happening for me. I saw how far YouTube could carry others, and I was desperate to get there, too.

One day, after spending hours trolling my competitors' sites, I complained to my mom about how everyone seemed to be doing better than me. As usual, her advice put things into perspective: "You need to slow down, Dulce. Take a step back and keep to your own path."

The media loves to tell stories of young people achieving incredible success or businesses that became phenomena seemingly overnight. How many times have you heard about the next big thing—whether it's a fresh-faced starlet, an unknown musician taking over the airwaves, or a hot new designer dominating fashion week? Here's the thing: The reason we hear these stories so often is because they are, in fact, extremely rare. No one cares about the guy who worked really hard for years and then achieved the success he wanted and lived happily ever after. That's not sexy, but it's still success.

Also, when you read stories about wildly successful people, you rarely hear about what they did before they were successful. Pick up any biography or memoir by someone famous, and inevitably, you will read a story of hard work, lucky breaks, and a lot of downs in between all those ups.

When I first started making my videos, every new follower and view felt like a major win. But a few years in, when I was getting thousands of followers and views on a single video, that alone no longer seemed like enough. I needed more to make me feel like a success. So how do you explain this weird shift? There's a concept in psychology called the hedonic treadmill. What it means is that the more we have of something, the more we end up wanting. Have you ever worked really hard toward a goal, only to achieve it and discover you still weren't satisfied? All of a sudden you were unhappy because, while you had one thing, you didn't have this other thing that was even better. This is especially true of material things—you may dream of living in a bigger house, but then, if you move in, you quickly start feeling like it's too small—but it's also true of success. You can achieve a goal you once only dreamed about—graduating college, starting your own business, landing your dream job—but soon you start seeing all the things other people have and you start wanting them, too.

If you're ambitious—and if you're reading this book, I know you are—you will likely always strive to be better. That's a great thing because it means you'll always want to grow. But when you don't allow yourself to be satisfied or when you constantly compare yourself to others, you'll never get to actually *enjoy* the sweet life.

There are a million ways to find success, and not all of them are obvious. The key is to listen to your heart and follow your passion. Everyone has his or her own innate set of talents, and in my experience, discovering them is half the battle. These days, tons of passionate, talented people are starting small businesses based solely on their interests rather than profit. Take Etsy, for example: The brilliant e-commerce platform makes it simple to launch an online store where you can sell all manner of one-of-a-kind creations. Contrary to popular belief, you don't need a lot of money to get started—a strong will and an Internet connection will do just fine.

We're all unique people with unique skills, interests, and hopes, so it makes perfect sense that our paths would be unique, too. Don't be discouraged if your path is windy and full of roadblocks while your peers seem to be gliding along smoothly. As long as you keep working to move forward, you'll get to where you need to be, no matter what.

Put Past Mistakes in Their Place

By the time I finished active duty in 2009, I felt like an entirely new person—a far cry from the troubled teenager of my youth.

Just as my YouTube channel was picking up steam, Jesse and I moved from Killeen, Texas, to Los Angeles, California, to be closer to our families. For years, I'd dreamed of following in Lauren Conrad's footsteps by attending the Fashion Institute of Design and Merchandising, or FIDM for short. Flipping through magazines and sketching in my free time was a great place to start, but it was about time I took my fashion education seriously.

FIDM's application process was a pretty major undertaking. In addition to the entrance essay and my high school records, I also had to submit an entrance project. It was a ton of work, but I was thrilled at the prospect of attending my dream school and anxiously awaited my acceptance letter. But it never came. Instead, I got a rejection letter telling me that even though I did well on the entrance project, my high school grades were not good enough for me to be admitted.

Unbelievable! After all that effort I'd put into moving on from my past, my earlier failures were coming back to haunt me. For so long I'd dreamed of attending FIDM, assuming it was going to take my career to the next level.

But now I had to face the fact that I never would realize that dream.

The old me might have gone into a negativity tailspin, telling myself I'd never be good enough, beating myself up for all the stupid things I did in high school. But the new me knew better, so I dusted myself off and applied to a different school, one that would give me a shot despite my crappy high school grades. I threw out FIDM's rejection and soon received an acceptance letter from the Art Institute of California—Hollywood. I was going to fashion school!

Though I didn't end up finishing my degree because my career got in the way, I did get to live out my dream of attending fashion school. My past has provided tons of valuable lessons that I still use to this day, but I didn't have to let it define my future. That's the thing about bad decisions and mistakes: You might be ready to forget them, but those pesky demons can come back to haunt you when you least expect it. Acknowledge them and then send them right back to the past where they belong.

Yes, I know it's so much easier said than done, and I still get sucked into the negativity spiral more than I care to admit. When I first got started, if a video didn't do well, my instinct was to go to a dark place and start preparing myself for the end of my YouTube career. Even now, a weak video has the power to make me feel like I am no longer relevant or good at what I do, and a bad business meeting can ruin my whole week. The key is not to dwell on those thoughts and to catch them before they get too loud. Because we've all made mistakes and not every venture will be a huge success, you just have to accept that things go wrong and move on.

Take Bite-Size Pieces

I've already told you about how, when I started basic training, I was hardly the picture of physical fitness. My biggest challenge was by far physical training. Specifically, I struggled with completing the sit-up and push-up exercises. While my fellow soldiers were dropping down and giving twenty like it was nothing, I could barely do five.

During one of our particularly grueling five a.m. exercise sessions, a drill sergeant named Sergeant Johnson saw that I was flailing and pulled me aside. Johnson, like the other drill sergeants, was incredibly tough and yelled a lot. This was the first time he'd singled me out, and I was pretty sure I was in for an earful about how my weakness was dragging down the entire platoon.

But instead of screaming, he comforted me. He said, "Even though you are struggling now, you're capable of doing just as many sit-ups and push-ups as the guys *if* you set your mind to it." In addition to the pep talk, he gave me an assignment: "Whenever you have free time, practice doing push-ups and sit-ups to train your body." He told me I had to take initiative when no one was looking to truly better myself. He promised that if I followed his plan, the next time I had physical training, I'd do better.

From that point on, every chance I had—a few minutes after making my bed, a moment of free time before lunch— I forced myself to practice. Each time, it got a little bit easier until I wasn't just passing the PT tests, I was outperforming guys twice my size!

This was my first lesson in breaking down big goals into tiny pieces. As I've said before, success does not happen overnight, and you can't expect to be perfect at something right from the get-go. Even amazingly talented people got that way by working in increments over time. Research has shown that in order to become exceptional at something— whether you're a ballet dancer, a concert pianist, a CEO, or a beauty vlogger—you need to practice it for ten thousand hours. That means, even if you work full-time at something, it will still take you a few years to master it.

Of course, if you start thinking about having to work at something for so long, the task can quickly become daunting. So instead of looking at the big picture, you need to break it down. I knew I couldn't just run a mile if I'd never run one before, and I knew I needed to be able to do five push-ups before I could do twenty. So, thanks to Sergeant Johnson's advice, I started breaking the goal down, and with enough time and dedicated practice, I became better.

Sometimes, it's much easier to put a goal into perspective if you visualize it. What I like to do is write what I want to accomplish in bold letters on a clean sheet of paper. Then, I write down five things that I know I can do to make that goal a reality. I apply the same concept to my career. Instead of working toward a goal of "rack up twenty thousand more followers on Instagram," I work toward posting a set amount of interesting and insightful Instagram posts every day. Taking bite-size chunks helps me tackle goals without feeling like I'm drowning, and I can finish each day with a sense of accomplishment. There is always work to do if you're working on something big, but I've learned that small victories accumulate into a much happier me.

Celebrate Small Accomplishments in a BIG Way

When you break things down into bite-size chunks, you'll immediately start feeling a fuller sense of accomplishment. Finishing one small task gets you that much closer to larger success. Celebrating the little victories you achieve as you go along is an important way to acknowledge your accomplishments.

When Izek was a baby, I would get incredibly stressed out by his baby bottles. Yes, you heard right. A sink full of baby bottles was enough to make me want to tear my hair out. There was no other option but to wash them, and I was washing them constantly to the point where my forearms would be sore. Each tiny bottle would have to be thoroughly scrubbed with an even tinier brush, only to have the bottles piled up in the sink just a couple of hours later. It felt like absolute madness to me.

Then, while skimming Pinterest one day, I saw a Dale Carnegie quote that struck me from the inside out. It said, "One grain of sand at a time." All I had to do was deconstruct that mass of baby bottles and think, "One bottle at a time." The next time it was my turn to wash those suckers, I looked at one bottle and gave it my full attention. Then, I moved on to the next and gave that bottle my full attention, too. When I was blind to the enormity of the situation (which, let's be honest, wasn't that enormous, but postpartum hormones can be gnarly), it was manageable! Before I knew it, I was done. And you better believe I celebrated! I did a little dance in my kitchen and gave myself permission to feel proud of this accomplishment, even though it was small. What I'm getting at is this: The victory is not as important as the way you *SEE* the situation. If you are always seeking out those big wins, you may miss the amazing things going on in your life every single day. If a project seems daunting, don't feel like you have to do it all in one shot. Set a goal, let yourself finish for the day, and don't forget to celebrate your win.

Harness the Power of Positive Thinking

In addition to meditation, I'm a big believer in the law of attraction. The concept is pretty simple: If you put out positive energy, you'll attract positive energy, and if you put out negative energy, well, you get the idea. I first learned about this simple formula when I discovered *The Secret,* by Rhonda Byrne, at twenty-six. If you haven't watched the movie or read the book, I highly recommend adding it to your must-read list (Oprah is a big fan, too!). From that point on, expressing gratitude not just for major things like family and success but also for smaller gifts like water, light, beauty, and nature became an integral part of my core belief system. The book helped open my eyes to see life's joys everywhere. It's such a simple shift in your mind-set, but when you allow yourself to live in the moment and be present, the power of positive thinking is virtually limitless.

Ever notice that it's so easy to complain about things that are actually blessings? In my case, having too much work, being stuck in traffic, or having to deal with cramps are some of my greatest hits. My faith helps me catch myself when I get into a negative mind-set. Instead of dwelling on the less desirable aspects of life, I spin them into positives: Having too much work is better than having no work; monthly pain indicates that my body is healthy and functioning properly. This commitment to gratitude has been priceless in my everyday life and my business. It's easy to get frustrated when things don't work out the way you planned, but having faith allows you to accept everything at face value. Rather than fixate on what you don't have, the opportunities you're not getting, or the things you can't control, think about how far you've come and the hard work you've put in to get there. This also applies to life in general. If you're anxiously waiting to be asked out on your first date, or stressing out about not receiving that college acceptance letter, just remember to stay positive: Everything will happen precisely when it's supposed to and how it's supposed to.

Chapter 4

Be Genuine: In a Sea of Others, There's Only One YOU

In the summer of 2010, I had been blogging for two years. My subscriber base had grown to 500,000 people and the Dulce Candy YouTube channel was generating more money than I had ever thought possible through ads and brand partnerships. But rather than take my success as it came and enjoy the incredible freedom it brought me to do what I love and to live comfortably, I wanted more. I became obsessed with growing my business to catch up to bloggers who had triple the subscribers I had and were getting big-time brand contracts. I noticed that the one unifying factor those girls had in common was a closet full of designer clothing and super expensive department store makeup. In my mind that's what was making them appealing not only to readers but to brands as well. So I figured that if I started purchasing and showing expensive things in my videos, I'd become as successful as they were.

When I first started making videos, the only makeup I could afford came from drugstores, not department stores. The clothes I wore for my style posts all came from mall stores like Forever 21, Wet Seal, and Charlotte Russe—places just about every girl has access to. I worked with what I had, and I loved every minute of it. People didn't have to spend a ton of cash to follow along with my makeup videos; odds are, most of the products I featured were already in their makeup drawers. But once I could afford more expensive products, and brands started offering me partnership opportunities and sending me fancy products to test—just like the big-name bloggers I wanted to be like—I got way too caught up in the glamour of it all. My hope was that if I started wearing the same high-end shoes, clothing, and handbags in my videos that the big-time girls were wearing in theirs, even more brands would take note.

What I didn't understand then was that for those girls, luxury was a part of their brand. Featuring expensive clothing and fancy products was what they had built their success on from day one. I had lost sight of the fact that I had built my brand on being relatable and featuring accessible products. Well, I've told you before that my viewers are a savvy bunch—they saw right through the charade and called me out on it.

Many of them have known me since I first started recording janky videos out of tiny rooms in Killeen, Texas, and South Central. My production values may have been poor, but they trusted that when I recommended a product or featured a new brand, I was being genuine. By swapping the affordable products in my videos for luxury brands and the Forever 21 outfits for high-end clothing, not only was I was not being true to myself, but I was losing my viewers' trust as well. Because getting brand partnerships was so new to me and I was so psyched to get their attention, I was saying yes to just about every opportunity without thinking through whether it was right for my brand. So obviously, when I collaborated with a makeup company on a wildly expensive makeup set ($125 for three pieces of makeup? What was I thinking!?), my viewers wanted nothing to do with it. Needless to say, that collaboration was a massive fail. All these deals and partnerships that I was agreeing to were absolutely useless without the support of my audience. I used to pride myself on giving my viewers what they wanted, but it seemed like I no longer knew what that was. And without an audience, what's the point of putting up videos?

Over the course of six months I lost sight of who I was. I lost all interest in making new videos and even dreaded going online. I had all the money I could possibly want but felt the opposite of happy or accomplished. I had to take a step back and reevaluate my priorities. I started thinking back to when I had felt the most on top of my game. That was when I was putting all of my energy toward producing content I could be proud of rather than tailoring it to what I thought would gain me the most popularity. The moment I made chasing popularity my goal, I stopped getting joy from my work and, consequently, lost the success I had worked so hard to get. I realized that I didn't have pride in my work when getting ahead was the driving factor. So I went back to creating content the way I used to, based on what my audience wanted to see, and my subscriber numbers started to grow again. But even more important than that, I felt like myself.

It's during these self-esteem lows that I often get caught up in comparing myself to others. Sure, having ambition and a healthy sense of competition is a powerful motivator. But as I've learned over and over in my career, looking to others for the secret formula for success doesn't get you far in the world of YouTube. Thinking you have to fit yourself into a preexisting mold to find success will get you absolutely nowhere. Just because others made it to the top using a specific approach doesn't mean the same approach will work for you. You'd be making a mistake in thinking there's no more room for new, innovative bloggers. Sure, there's already one Michelle Phan and one Jenna Marbles, but there's also only ONE of you! The Internet is as vast and wide as deep space. There's plenty of room for everyone; you just have to find your own unique way to get there.

Real People Respond to Real People

....

The people who make it big on YouTube are the ones who are the most authentic. Some people have a funny personality, some can wax poetic about high-end designers, while others are all about budget finds and DIY. There's an audience for whoever you are. Ask yourself: "What can I offer? What's special/interesting/relevant/charming about me that will keep people coming back?" The beauty of the Internet is that it's limitless; there's something to pique the interests of absolutely everyone. There are beauty bloggers who build entire channels around their unique hair textures, specific skin tones, or a deep love of glitter. There are comedians, science enthusiasts, comic book nerds, fashion addicts, and foodies. Odds are, if you have a specific interest or demand, someone on YouTube is meeting it. And if there isn't, do it yourself!

Being authentic in my videos helped me connect with viewers who were starting to drift away, but that genuine spirit has had a ripple effect in the rest of my life, too, to some pretty amazing results. I learned that being genuine is important. I learned that it is in fact much easier to be genuine than not. I learned that people can smell a fake from a mile away, and I learned that something as simple as being true to my authentic self could make me happy beyond measure. It took a little while for me to learn how to pull it off, but once I did, I started to feel more comfortable in my own skin, which, in turn, helped others feel more at ease around me.

I've always looked up to my little sister, Wendy. She's never had an iota of insecurity and makes every decision by listening to her gut. Wendy doesn't let other people make her feel bad about herself, and she only answers to the voice in her own head. My sister has always been this way: She'd defend her friends against bullies, and she'd plainly and unapologetically state that she would rather be at home with her family when invited to hang out with the popular crowd. She's always danced to the beat of her own drum. I never gave myself the permission to have that type of freedom because of my chronic insecurity, so I've always admired her for it. When I ask her how she's always been so true to who she is, she shrugs her shoulders and says, "That's just me." I've learned to shrug my shoulders and be me, too.

Being Yourself Is Easier Than Being Someone Else

When I make my videos, it's pretty easy for me to relax and be myself because no one is watching. Well, at least no one is watching as I'm shooting and editing the videos. I know after I post them, millions of people will be able to see them, but for me, that's much different from getting up in front of a room full of people or meeting someone for the first time.

Because I'm naturally shy, I used to always put up a veneer when meeting new people. I was constantly worried people would see my flaws and decide they didn't want to associate with me. At my core, I am friendly but not hyper. I am curious but not especially talkative. I am kind but not overly complimentary. But I would approach people I didn't know with my best face forward, acting hyper, bubbly, and extra complimentary. People gravitate toward outgoing, over-the-top personalities (I know I did), so I thought that my put-on, over-the-top personality was more likable than my real personality. I would be all smiles, and my voice would jump at least two octaves (veering into shrill territory). I felt like I was in a pageant.

After about a year or two on YouTube, I started getting more recognition and people would actually come up to me on the street. I'd immediately turn "on." A viewer or fan would approach me, and it'd be perma-smile central! There were no genuine connections made, to say the least, and I'd walk around praying that I wouldn't be recognized, in hopes of avoiding the stressful situation altogether. Being someone else is exhausting. It takes a ton of mental energy to worry about whether someone will like you as you are. Being yourself? Now that's easy. I have a naturally shy disposition, and it takes a little while for me to ease up and settle in. That's me!

Now that I'm more comfortable in my own skin, I love putting myself in situations to test just how genuine I can be, even when under pressure. In May 2014, I was scheduled to be on *Good Morning America* to promote BeautyCon, a huge beauty summit that brings hundreds of digital influencers together with thousands of fans. Needless to say, thinking about appearing on live television in front of thirty million viewers made me very nervous. I was convinced that I needed to be bright and shiny and fun or no one else would want me to appear on their show ever again. I sought out counsel from a publicist and my manager. Their advice was simple: "Be yourself." So when I went onto *Good Morning America*, I decided to try just that. I dropped the veneer, and when those bright studio lights came on, and I felt that rush of crazy adrenaline, I took a deep breath and stared into the camera.

Miraculously, I was myself. I was friendly, just as I am in real life. I stayed low-key, calm, and even-keeled. I was genuine. I talked about BeautyCon and my channel the way I would talk about those topics with my friends. I went into my segment about a sun-kissed bronzer look and did a quick tutorial on one of the producers. It was just like shooting a video in my office back home. The positive feedback I received afterward was amazing. I got e-mails from my fellow YouTubers who told me that I stole the show. My family, who were watching from home, said that I was a natural. Those words of encouragement gave me the confidence to keep being myself. And it trickled into the rest of my NYC business trip.

After the *GMA* shoot, I was scheduled to have a business dinner with a brand to discuss a potential collaboration. Normally, this type of meeting would make me feel absolutely bonkers. I would worry that I wouldn't know what to talk about and cringe at the thought of the inevitable awkward silences. For me, going to a dinner with people I didn't know was about as stressful as going onstage and having to put on an impromptu show. But riding the high of my appearance on *GMA*, I was able to carry that new genuine attitude to the meeting. I was still a little anxious, but when I saw them waiting for me in the lobby of my hotel, I didn't feel that tightness in my chest or the knot in the pit of my stomach. I remembered how easy things had been for me when I remained true to who I am.

While we walked over to the restaurant a couple of blocks down the street, I noticed that Sarah, one of the people on the marketing team, was walking quietly without really engaging in conversation, so I made the choice to strike up a conversation with her. I asked if she had ever been to the restaurant before, and she immediately started chatting with me. I realized that, if I relaxed a little bit and took a bit of friendly initiative, I could dramatically change an interaction.

Sarah and I chatted on the walk there, and I got to feel like I was actually going to enjoy myself instead of being worried about the business portion of the evening. During our two-hour dinner, I formed some real bonds within the group. They asked me about what it was like growing up as an immigrant and my time in Iraq. I talked about marriage and being a mom. They talked about work and living in a big city. We all talked about how hard it is to balance a crazy career and a personal life. All these topics would be off-limits had I been putting up a front. I let myself be real, and when that happened, I attracted people who I would get along with in real life. Finding these kinds of connections is the best part of being true to oneself, and I found myself thoroughly enjoying the conversations that night. So I'll pass along the same advice that my manager and publicist gave me: Be yourself! You'll be more comfortable and you'll attract the types of people you'll want to be friends with for a long, long time.

Building Your Brand

After I spent a couple of years building an archive of videos, brands began approaching me with partnership opportunities more frequently. Companies like L'Oréal wanted me to represent them, and shows like *Good Morning America* wanted me to share my opinions. These household names wanted to be associated with me, and I began to realize that my YouTube hobby was more than just a pastime. I had become a brand.

Most of us think of a brand as something invented by advertisers or something that requires constant attention and curating. It's a strange feeling to think that your life is marketable and monetizable—but I promise it's not as uncommon as you think! Think about it—what defines a brand? A brand is unique to a specific product and influences the way consumers feel about it. Are you loyal to any particular brands? There are hundreds of different eye shadow brands on the market, but I particularly love Benefit and Too Faced. I've tried a lot of great products, but I know whenever I buy something from them, it's going to be quality, will match my personality, and will be worth the price. If there was no brand, I'd never be able to distinguish between products; the brand helps me identify what I want quickly.

The same is true of people. If you're applying for a job, there are likely dozens (if not hundreds or thousands) of other people vying for the same one, most, if not all, of whom are just as qualified for the position as you are. To get people to notice your résumé, let alone hire you, you need to stand out. I don't mean you need to dip your résumé in chocolate or hire an airplane to wave a banner over the place you want to work, extolling all of your virtues. What I mean is, you need your potential employer to see why you're special, how you have something extra, something unique to you that makes you the best person for the job. That, my friends, is your brand.

BRAND BUILDING, PART I:
KNOW WHAT MAKES YOU DIFFERENT

The first part of brand building starts with your self-esteem. Think about how salespeople and marketers talk about the brands they represent. It is their job to have a clear vision of what they are selling, and have the confidence to believe that they are selling something good. The best brands stand for something beyond the product they sell, and know exactly who they're marketing to. Apple is for cool kids, Microsoft is for business types—and the same is true for you.

I always take the time to curate my brand and make sure I don't lose sight of what makes me different. Think about it this way: If you were selling a product, you'd make a list of all of its attributes in order to position it to sell. This mission statement will help you verbalize what you stand for. Are you a facilitator? A workhorse? A creative leader? What do you have to offer that separates you from the pack? My words include "Latina," "beauty and fashion authority," "motivational," "mother," and "veteran." These words have helped me navigate the direction I'd like to steer my brand and remind me of the different facets that I represent and the types of people I'd like to reach.

Remember to be yourself. You can't define your brand based on a vision of what you think you *should* be but, rather, of what you are. Even if you see that there's a market for elephant-training videos on YouTube, do not try to become an elephant trainer just because you think you might attract attention. Or maybe YouTube isn't your thing at all. Maybe you don't like posting videos online. If that's the case but you want to express yourself, try writing a blog.

Another important point to keep in mind is that your brand isn't limited to what makes you money. Your brand is the total sum of who you are—embrace all of the things that make you into a unique individual and incorporate them into your brand.

BRAND BUILDING, PART II: CRAFT YOUR PITCH

As awkward as it may initially be, you've got to be able to talk about yourself like you're worth it! It was hard for me in the beginning, too. Talking about myself, let alone praising myself, felt absolutely unnatural. It can seem boastful or even arrogant. But if you don't believe in your own brand, then why should anyone else?

An easy way to get comfortable with talking about yourself is to know your accomplishments through and through. Write down the stuff that you think is worthwhile about yourself and be generous! When creating a list of your accomplishments, don't just write down the actions but write down the outcome of the action, too. For instance, don't write,

"Led four people on a team." Instead, write, "Led four people on a team to implement a new work-flow process that helped save the company $500,000." See? The outcome is way more interesting than simply stating what you did. Know what you've accomplished and believe that those accomplishments are damn impressive.

My secret: Have a document on hand (you can have a physical piece of paper or save one on your computer) where you keep a running list of milestones. Every time something major happens or you accomplish an impressive task, add to it. I usually include the date, the people involved, the outcome, and even the way I felt, because sometimes that can help trigger my memory or add color to the story. On this list, I have everything from winning my PT contest in Iraq to being one of *Glamour* magazine's Most Influential Women in 2013. My experiences run the gamut, but if I ever need to talk about myself, I have this trusty list, and it helps me feel proud but not egotistical—it's just a list of facts, after all. Plus, it's been so helpful for this book (and I didn't even know I was going to write one when I started the list!).

BRAND BUILDING, PART III:
DON'T HIDE YOUR MISTAKES

One of the most important attributes of any brand is trust. This means you need to be honest. In order to become a trustworthy brand, it's important to own up to your mistakes. While it's great to nail down talking about all of your accomplishments, keep in mind that your failures matter just as much. The way we bounce back from the bad stuff makes us into well-rounded people. It's an admirable quality to be able to spin a difficult situation into a learning one, and part of being a great employee, a fabulous employer, or a hard-working student is the ability to mature and grow from negative experiences.

Keep a couple of these examples of growth close to you. If you're in a job interview and the interviewer asks you to talk about a situation where the outcome wasn't what you expected, you will have a great answer! Failure is an important part of success, and branding yourself as infallible can only come back to bite you later on. It is a fact that you and I will fail. Everyone fails. Even the anticipation of failure can be off-putting. But once you accept that it will undoubtedly happen, it will be that much easier to handle when it comes your way. The most important thing is to spin it to be positive.

And if you have to, apologize. Knowing how to own up and say you're sorry—and mean it—if you say something offensive or hurt someone unintentionally will only make you better.

BRAND BUILDING, PART IV:
PROTECT YOUR BRAND

Everything you make public about yourself is like sending out a press release for your brand. Press releases are carefully crafted to communicate information in a controlled, smart way so that, even if bad news has to be delivered, it sounds as positive as possible. If you've branded yourself so that people believe you are responsible and trustworthy, you wouldn't write a press release about that crazy party you went to last weekend or spread gossip about one of your coworkers.

The Internet makes it incredibly easy for anyone to look up information about you that you might not want them to see. And that's the cost of living in a world that's so reliant on the Internet and social media. Anything you put up—a picture, a blog post, a status update—is public and therefore instantly becomes part of your brand. Don't forget, once something is online, it's very hard—even impossible, in some cases—to erase it or take it down.

So be smart about it and curate your persona carefully. I've touched on this multiple times throughout the book, but remember that it's when you are your most authentic self that you attract the people and situations that work for you. It's when you are true to yourself that the types of people you want to work with, or be friends with, come your way. With on what your brand promised and conduct yourself in a professional way. For me, that means showing up on time, taking my work seriously, and thinking big picture. How will this partnership be mutually beneficial? Every effort helps. I can promise that as you get older, the world seems to get smaller and smaller. Your friend will have a cousin who works at your dream job, or your intern may become your boss someday. So whatever you put out into the world, make sure not only that it's authentic and true but also that you exude kindness and respect to absolutely everyone. Think about it: When a company has done a really good job with a product, people talk about it even in the absence of advertising. That's how you know you have a successful brand. It exists on its own and people will promote it for you. This should be your goal as well. The best way to make sure that you are indispensable is to be, well, indispensable. People will vouch for you if they think you'll make them look good. Educate yourself on the ins and outs of your job. Figure out how to help the company save time or money, or how to make your boss's life easier—he or she is bound to sing your praises. If you're in school, take advantage of the amazing opportunities to meet new people to impress. Show them you're willing to learn and work your tail off! In any case, it's marketing 101: Create a buzz and get people talking.

For me, I try and create a buzz for my "customers." My situation is unique in that I have two sets of customers: There are my viewers, who are the backbone of my business (so my main goal is to keep creating content they will love), and then there are the sponsors and companies that make it possible for me to keep creating that awesome content. It's a delicate ecosystem to balance. I want to make sure both sets of people are happy, and I try my hardest to make sure all parties involved are satisfied. For my viewers, I make sure to be consistent. It all starts with asking them what they want to see. And as I said before, Dulce Candy viewers are super savvy. They respond with some amazingly creative ideas. The videos are ultimately for them, so of course I take their sound advice. When I create a video, I always give 100 percent. I never ever half-ass a video. I give as many hours as needed, whether in the research, filming, or editing process. I ask myself, "Is there a way to make this better?" Oftentimes, there are tweaks I can make to elevate the project. I'll take the extra time to make it right because I want to offer my viewers the best of me. They know that they can expect two quality videos a week and an accompanying blog post, along with vlogs on my daily-life channel.

The companies I work with know that I will meet the deadlines they set for me and the work will be up to a certain standard. I want to make sure they see me as an influential partner who can keep up her end of the deal. I remember to be flexible and build close relationships with these companies so I can do bigger and better things on my channel. And if you're in a unique position like I am, it's not much different from the advice I've laid out in this chapter. I allow

Not Everyone Will Accept You— and That's Okay

Toward the end of my active duty time in Killeen, Texas, I had been posting YouTube videos for about three months. Because I started shooting them with zero expectations, I was absolutely thrilled when the videos began gaining traction. I was getting more and more return viewers, and my subscriber numbers were steadily climbing. My co-workers at the motor pool had no idea what I was up to on my time off. Honestly, I was a little embarrassed to tell them. They already knew that I loved makeup a lot more than I liked working on generators and constantly teased me about it.

My unexpected success gave me a surge of confidence to share my new hobby. Their response was not at all what I thought it would be. I wasn't expecting them to praise my efforts or whip out their laptops to watch along as I gushed about eye shadow and lip gloss, but I did think they'd be proud or at least impressed that *other* people were watching. Instead of compliments, my new project was met with complete indifference. I didn't get it—weren't we supposed to be family? And isn't family supposed to support one another no matter what? Of course a little teasing is to be expected between "siblings," but not only were they unsupportive of my interests outside the military, they also put down my decision not to reenlist every chance they got. "Girls like you don't make it out there in the real world" and "You'll come crawling back to the army after you see what it's really like out there" were words I heard pretty much daily.

I was, of course, hurt by their insensitivity to my passions, but I refused to let their words keep me down. I was enjoying making videos and my mind was made up—I was going to leave the army, and I wasn't going to let their negativity ruin my plan to follow my dream. When my last day at the motor pool finally came, I had given up hope that they'd come around or support my decision to pursue my new interests. In fact, very few actually wished me luck or even hugged me good-bye. For the most part, what I got were a bunch of snarky comments like "You'll be back" or "See you later, Tejeda!"

I realize now that the remarks I got from my fellow soldiers, though unpleasant and hurtful, weren't coming from a bad place. In their own way, they were trying to protect me from the outside world. And believe me, there was a part of me that thought they might be right. Staying in the army was definitely the safer way to go. But seeing that initial growth on my channel was proof that I was onto something and that I owed it to myself to explore the possibilities.

On your way to success, you are bound to make decisions that those closest to you—parents, teachers, or friends— won't understand. Rather than burn a bridge or write them off, explain your motivations and tell them you have to follow your dreams, whether they see it as the right thing to do or not. At the end of the day the really important people will love you no matter what. Their intentions, though maybe poorly expressed, are coming from a good place. And if some people still don't understand, if they still put you down, then they'll never accept you for who you are and it's best to drop the subject with them altogether and avoid unnecessary disappointment. And whatever you do, DO NOT let these people's negativity steer you away from your dreams.

Real People Don't Respond to Fakes

I've saved this subject for last because it's one of the hardest concepts for anyone to master. Being genuine means showing other people who you are, as you *really* are. Your voice, your expressions, your movements, your opinions . . . you aren't hiding the person you are when no one is watching—imperfections included. It's only natural to want to put up a front, but I've learned the hard way that the response you get for being an honest-to-goodness real person creates lasting relationships.

In other words, in order to be truly sincere, you need to allow yourself to be vulnerable. Vulnerability is a scary idea, right? At least, it is for me. It's like putting yourself out there and saying, "This is the real me, take it or leave it!" It's when you put yourself out there that the fear of rejection can set in. But I must say, this is a great way to weed out the people who don't belong in your life anyway. If someone can't accept the most straightforward version of you, that relationship might not be worth pursuing.

You can also take this a step further than just being yourself. Have you ever been hanging out with a friend when she told you something deeply personal about herself? Maybe she told you a secret and was nervous because she worried you'd judge her? How did you feel afterward? You probably felt even closer to her than you were before. She opened her heart to you, and as a result you built a connection. Maybe you shared something with her in exchange to help her feel better and more at ease.

Vulnerability allows us to be honest about who we are, and when we're honest, we allow other people to know us even better. Without vulnerability, we could never form deep, lasting relationships. Can you imagine what it would feel like if you had no one in your life you could cry to? Maybe you can, in which case, I hope you find someone in your life to open up to. Back in high school, I felt like I had no one to talk to about my problems. Of course, I was surrounded by people who wanted to help, but because I was embarrassed, I didn't let myself be vulnerable. As a result, my suffering lasted way longer than it should have.

Nowadays, I try to make vulnerability part of my job. I talk about my life and personal demons on my channel, and I've written about a lot of them here. I am so lucky to have amazing interactions with my fans during meet-and-greets. And because it's so quick-paced (introduction, picture, hug, and then good-bye), I can't sit down and have the types of meaningful conversations I'd want with each and every viewer who takes time out of their day to come see me. When I meet the fans who watch my videos and support me, there is no awkwardness between us. They know so much about me—and I know so much about my audience—that it doesn't feel like I'm meeting strangers. And because they give me genuine love, it's easy to reciprocate that level of enthusiasm. Sometimes, though, the level of closeness astounds me.

One of those instances was when I got a message from a viewer named Suzy. Suzy mailed me a pink card with a simple design on the front. When I got the envelope in the mail, I expected a typical fan letter saying how much she loved my videos (which, don't get me wrong, I love getting!). But this card was different. Suzy explained that she was a twenty-three-year-old woman battling ovarian cancer, one of the deadliest forms of the disease. "I'm a mom and losing my hair from intense chemotherapy," Suzy wrote. She went on to tell me that she watched my videos to get through her toughest days.

With just one letter, she solidified my purpose. Despite the apparent frivolity of what I do, I was able to connect with someone as a friend. I put my honest, genuine, and vulnerable self out there, which, in turn, helped someone else feel comfortable enough to be vulnerable with me. By being myself, and using beauty to connect with real people, I can make a difference—and it's an honor to be able to parlay my job into something more meaningful. Suzy is someone going through a really difficult time, and to play a tiny part in making her day a bit better is beyond what I'm even able to express in words. To this day (and for the long haul), the card is posted up on my mirror and it serves as my motivation. I look at it every morning. And on days that I don't feel like I'm good enough, her words validate what I'm doing. That card lets me know that no matter what happens, I should keep working. If my genuine self can be a distraction or a joy to even just a handful of people, I'll be happy. Suzy took important time out of her day to validate *my* purpose. I'll always be thankful to her for that and for the thousands of other fans who reach out to me time and time again.

Chapter 5

Make Fear Your BFF

A couple of years ago, I was presented with an opportunity to be an ambassador for CoverGirl, one of the largest cosmetics companies in the world. This was by far the biggest brand that had ever approached me before, and I was instantly overcome with memories of watching the iconic commercials on TV. The joy I felt evaporated the minute I learned that, contractually, my duties included conducting red carpet interviews during the 2013 Teen Choice Awards. I would have to get dolled up and join professional reporters on the red carpet to interview celebrities about their hair and makeup. Those interviews would be broadcast on TV to give the viewers at home a peek at the behind-the-scenes action. Two of my Latina idols, Jessica Alba and Jennifer Lopez, were on the guest list.

When I read the e-mail outlining the requirements, my stomach did somersaults. I had zero media training. I'd never talked to a real celebrity in my life. I imagined tripping and falling on my face in front of Jessica and Jennifer (and, worse, taking them down with me). I pictured myself stuttering on camera while trying to talk to Katy Perry and forgetting my questions. I was sure that I would make a giant mess of the event and CoverGirl would see that they had made a mistake by teaming up with an amateur like me.

The doubts and worst-case scenarios swept over me like a tsunami—and I was drowning in negative thoughts. After reading the e-mail a few more times, I drafted a reply to the CoverGirl marketing team. "I'm sorry," I wrote. "I have another engagement that evening." Just like that, I no longer had to worry about making a fool of myself on TV . . . and I also no longer had a partnership with CoverGirl.

My replacement for the Teen Choice Awards red carpet job was another YouTuber, a friend of mine with whom I have a lot in common in both our professional and personal lives. The day of the awards ceremony, I settled in to watch the preshow interviews from the comfort of my couch. My friend popped up on screen in a smoking-hot gown and incredible hair and makeup. She nailed the interviews like she'd been doing live TV her whole life! I watched her—someone who wasn't any more qualified for the job than I was—take on the challenge with confidence and grace. She wasn't a professional anchor, but she got out there and chatted up those A-listers like a pro. If she could do it, why couldn't I?

Fear has always played a significant role in my life. I'm not proud of it, but I have done some crazy things in my life to get out of doing something I was afraid of. In high school, I flunked a homework assignment on purpose to avoid getting up in front of the class to give an oral presentation (public speaking is still something I struggle with). But the CoverGirl incident showed me that, by avoiding things I was afraid of, I would miss out on a lot, not to mention skip amazing opportunities that could help my brand and career expand. This experience taught me a few valuable lessons about the role fear can play in our lives.

There Are Two Types of Fear, and Both Are Blessings in Disguise

When I was in Iraq, I experienced true, bone-rattling fear. Whether it was the RPGs (rocket-propelled grenades) that would land in our camp without warning, or when my then boyfriend—now husband—Jesse would venture out on dangerous missions for weeks at a time, I have been in fear for my life and the safety of someone I loved.

During the last four months of my deployment, the unrest in Iraq became much more palpable. When I first got to Iraq, mortar attacks were a once-a-month occurrence, but toward the end of my tour, they were coming in almost daily and in larger quantities. One morning, I was in my trailer getting ready for breakfast after my workout when the alarm started blaring: "Incoming! Incoming! Incoming!" followed by "Take cover! Take cover! Take cover!" Before I had the chance to react, the ground started to shake. My things were falling off the shelves, and I could hear excruciatingly loud booms all around me. I saw my fellow soldiers running and dropping to the ground, their faces twisted with horror. There was a barrier outside each trailer made out of concrete and steel that served as protection during attacks. I snapped out of my shock and made my way to the barrier to hide. This was the first time since I'd arrived that I actually thought I was going to die. All I could do was shut my eyes, like I did when I was a little girl crossing the border. I thought that if I didn't see what's happening, it couldn't hurt me.

Being so close to an attack made me confront mortality head-on. There was nowhere safe, and bad things could happen at any time. For a while after I got back to the States, I suffered from PTSD. Loud noises such as helicopters and car horns would make me jump and duck for cover. I distinctly remember when a magnitude 3.5 earthquake hit in the middle of the night, my immediate reaction was to roll out of bed and crouch, waiting for the next mortar to hit.

Fear is a good and natural feeling. Fear allows us to

recognize and avoid danger, prevent ourselves or people we love from doing something that could cause them harm, and flee when threatened. If we were never afraid, we'd end up walking into dangerous situations completely unaware of what was in store. Without fear, I might not have survived Iraq because my instinct to duck and cover would never have kicked in. In life-threatening circumstances, fear is a blessing that allows us to survive.

But there is a flip side. Eventually, I started to readjust to life at home and the fear I experienced in Iraq was replaced with something different. You'd think that spending time in a war zone would have made me pretty fearless, but even though I was completely safe from imminent threats, I was still plagued by a different kind of fear—perceived fear.

Perceived fear is what we feel when we get out of our comfort zone. It's an extension of the other type of fear we feel when our lives are in danger, but instead of being caused by a very real threat, it is often only real in our minds. I know rationally that the things I'm scared of now—being on camera, doing a photo shoot in front of strangers—are not actually dangerous, but that doesn't stop me from fearing them.

For a while, I let these fears dictate my life. I didn't want to accept work opportunities, I didn't want to take on large projects, and I didn't even want to meet important people. It was so much easier going through life that way. But I knew deep down, by staying in my comfort zone, I was denying myself happiness and, more importantly, growth.

dulce candy ruiz

The Only Way to Overcome Fear
Is to Stare It in the Face

After the CoverGirl debacle, I had resolved to say yes to projects that came my way and deal with the aftereffects like a professional. That's not to say that I was no longer a fear-driven person, but I realized that I needed to embrace fear if I was ever going to take my career to the next level.

I'm glad I figured this out when I did because a few weeks later *Project Runway* called and asked me to appear on one of the episodes. I immediately accepted.

As luck would have it, the production team needed me in New York to shoot the following day, which meant there was no time to get in my head and psych myself out. I was one of several people called in to represent a "real girl" in the episode. The contestants' challenge was to design a look based on our personal style and taste, and at the end of the show, we "real girls" were required to model the final designs on the famous catwalk.

I'm usually a deer in headlights when I'm in front of the camera, and *Project Runway* had more than five cameras pointed my way. If ever there was a time to stare my fear in the face, this was it. Imagine dozens of crew members, designers, and judges (not just any ol' judges—I'm talking Nina Garcia, Christian Siriano, Isaac Mizrahi, and Alyssa Milano) staring you up and down while you try to get to the end of the catwalk in one piece.

Fun fact: Thanks to the magic of editing, by the time the show aired, the models are on the runway for only a few moments. In reality, I walked up and down that catwalk over and over—in dead silence—so the cameramen could get their shot. Then, I was asked to stand very still at the end of the runway, smile big, and pose for two minutes. That may not sound like a lot of time, but when you have to stand like a statue while everyone in the room judges you (literally!), two minutes can seem like a lifetime. "Nervous" doesn't even begin to describe how I felt before getting on that runway.

Maybe it was the realization that doing uncomfortable things would benefit me in the long run, but when I was getting ready backstage (and terrified out of my mind), my survival instincts kicked in. I don't know where the thought came from exactly, but out of nowhere, I started to repeat this mantra to myself: "You're confident and you're beautiful . . . you're confident and you're beautiful . . . you're confident and you're beautiful . . ." By the time I got on set, those words were playing in my head on a permanent loop.

A couple of weeks later the episode aired and guess what? I did indeed look confident and beautiful! It was a life-changing epiphany for me. I realized that if I just acknowledged my fears and insecurities, then I could overcome all the negative thoughts invading my brain that were trying to take me down. This requires believing in yourself, and knowing that you're worthy of the opportunities given to you.

Say Yes to Things That Scare You

These days, I use fear as a gauge: The bigger the fear, the bigger the opportunity for growth! Instead of avoiding such situations, I embrace and even welcome them. Fear lets me know that something truly amazing could be around the corner. Like writing a book, for example. The thought of doing this, I'm not ashamed to say, freaked me out big-time! But I'm so glad I did it because it's been an amazing, one-of-a-kind experience that the old me would have run far away from. It's not that the fear has gone away completely—I think it will always be there in some respect. But I've learned to be less afraid to take calculated risks. Just about every aspect of my life can benefit from this philosophy, be it career, relationships, or even spirituality.

It's so easy to think of fear as a negative thing, and it's equally as easy to get caught up in everyday fears (some of mine include: "Will I get a nasty comment on a video?" or "Will I sound like a dork in an interview?"). But I've found that if you use fear as a barometer to tell you what you *should* do instead of what you shouldn't do, you'll be amazed at how many opportunities you have that didn't exist before.

You can tell a good opportunity from a bad one if it scares you in the best way possible. A good opportunity will give you butterflies in your stomach because it's a new and exciting challenge. You will be scared, but eager to dive in and get started. With a good opportunity, you will feel a sense of urgency to give it all you've got.

When my vlog was starting to make some headway with small-time makeup brands, Coach approached me to do a holiday giveaway. I had never worked with a luxury brand before, and from my tiny, run-down living room in South Central, Los Angeles, I felt like I was living the very opposite of a luxurious lifestyle. It was the first time that a luxury brand had come to me, so I was extraordinarily anxious about disappointing them with the outcome. My self-doubt was creeping in again, and I was ready to say no for all the wrong reasons.

This opportunity scared me, but I couldn't stop the ideas from coming. I was excited about the concept and was even more thrilled to be able to give away a really lovely gift to my viewers. I took that as a sign that I should move forward with the partnership. So I came up with a fun script, shot the video (over and over again to get it perfect), and spent days editing, wondering if the video was going to be a success. The giveaway turned out to be a runaway hit and was the catalyst for several collaborations I did with other big-name brands like Macy's and L'Oréal. Thanks, Coach, for taking a chance on me! I learned that saying yes to projects that scare me is a good way to light a fire under my butt to go above and beyond what I originally thought I was capable of.

You *Can* Train Yourself to Be Confident

I discovered a great book while researching confidence and self-esteem. It's called *The Confidence Code,* by Katty Kay and Claire Shipman. According to the book, some people are born naturally confident while others are not. And even though I definitely do NOT possess that magical gene, the authors argue that, luckily, confidence is a skill that can be learned. Kay and Shipman suggest that even though you can't fake confidence, you can acquire it over time by taking risks and powering through insecurities. For me, the key was to pinpoint the situations in which I felt the most insecure, then figure out a way to handle them better. After I started paying attention, I discovered my weakest moments were all centered around fear, things like doing a massive photo shoot or saying no to a partnership I knew was the wrong fit for my brand. But when I began viewing the weak moments as opportunities, I was able to face my fears head-on and, as a result, gradually became more and more confident. You possess the power to do anything you set your mind to. If you exercise it, you'll feel, well . . . powerful! And there's nothing more beautiful than inner strength.

Fear and self-consciousness have a way of sneaking up on you unless you keep them in check. Here are the three ways I make sure I keep my confidence levels high at all times.

Don't Become Complacent—Rather than get too comfortable with how far I've come, I continue to challenge myself. This means regularly agreeing to opportunities that scare me or force me out of my comfort zone. I don't think I'll ever feel 100 percent comfortable doing live television, red carpet interviews, or public speaking—which is precisely why it's so important for me to keep doing them!

Repeat Positive Affirmations—I don't go by one trusty mantra. Instead, I make up new ones to custom-fit the specific situation or challenge I'm faced with. If it's a TV appearance, I might psych myself up by repeating "You're confident and you're beautiful" over and over. If it's an interview, I'll most likely prep by telling myself "Don't be scared, you got this" while getting ready in the green room. Even if it's something as simple as a photo shoot with a team of people I've never worked with before, I calm myself by repeating "It's going to be fun day, and you'll do a great job" and "If my higher power didn't think I could do this, he wouldn't place this opportunity in front of me" before I go to bed the night before. This way, I wake up with a positive mind-set and ready to take on the day, and the constant loop of positivity crowds out the negative thoughts that would otherwise creep into my head.

Know Your Triggers—This is a big one, guys. As hard as I've worked not to let the haters get the best of me, the judgment and negativity I get online is still one of my biggest confidence crushers. Sure, the negative comments don't affect me the way they used to, but I'm always cognizant of the steady stream of negativity coming my way. Being judged is an occupational hazard for me, one I've grown to accept. But still, it's on me to make sure I don't get caught up in all the hostility by understanding that the negativity has a lot more to do with the person who is sending it my way than with my own shortcomings.

Fake It Till You Make It

Fun fact: Simply changing your body language can make you appear confident even if you're not. Because I'm four foot nine, I've always had a tiny (ha!) bit of a Napoleon complex. My dad must have anticipated a tough road ahead for me because when I was in junior high school, he taught me the importance of posture. Pulling my shoulders back, tilting my chin upward, and holding my head up high are great ways to fake the appearance of unshakable confidence. I followed his advice and miraculously never got bullied. I noticed that the kids who got called names or, even worse, shoved into lockers kept their heads down, their eyes cast to the ground, and their shoulders scrunched forward. They looked like victims, as though they were expecting to be messed with. This was my first lesson in the importance of body language. Though I didn't have high self-esteem during junior high and high school, I'd apparently fooled everyone else into thinking that I did.

To me, body language is like a costume—a way to present yourself to others that's easily changeable. The body language that you adopt says a lot about you, especially when you meet someone for the first time. The way you move is an indicator of the energy you feel, and conversely, sometimes changing your movements can influence your mental state, too. When I first walked into my fashion marketing class at the Art Institute, my instinct was to make a beeline for the back of the lecture hall. I hadn't been in school in a long time, and even in high school, I felt most at home fading into the background. As I made my way through the classroom's double doors, I saw the faces and heard the voices of my old army comrades who said they were sure I wouldn't be able to make it in the civilian world. I needed to prove them wrong. So instead of hiding in the back, I remembered what my father had taught me. I walked to the front row and sat down. I challenged myself to speak up that day, and what do you know? My classmates perceived me as confident and knowledgeable. They even asked for my advice on projects and ran their ideas by me. For the first time, I actually felt smart in school—as if I had something valuable to contribute—and all I'd had to do was pick a different seat and raise my hand a few times. The power of body language indeed!

Fear of Success

I've come to terms with the fact that the key to dealing with setbacks is to bounce back. I've dealt with anxiety, stage fright (I'm taking a Toastmasters class as I write this), and, of course, my fear of failure. But what do you do when an entirely different fear sets in, the kind that hits on a deeper level? I'm talking about the fear of success that so often holds people back. Even armed with the knowledge that better things are to come, leaving my comfort zone to achieve those things has always been a major challenge. I've always been aware that success would come with its own set of new demands, and quite frankly, I dreaded taking them on. Just think of it this way: You finally get that promotion you've been after, and you couldn't be more proud. But then the fear of success sets in—the realization that now you have to actually *do* the job and take on all the new challenges and responsibilities that come with it: "Did I push myself too far? Am I even capable of handling this job? What if it turns out I've just been lucky this whole time and everyone discovers I'm a total fraud?"

I think the answer to this unique fear is twofold. Firstly, it's to tell yourself that it's never as bad as you've made it out to be. How often have you been presented with a problem and found that you were overwhelmed even before attacking it? It happens to me all the time. And by the time I've solved the problem/finished the project/worked through the issue, I find myself saying, "Ah, that wasn't so bad." We often don't give ourselves enough credit. Give yourself permission to be successful: Chances are, you're the only one who believes you're not capable. The second part of working through the fear of success is to surround yourself with people whom you respect and consider to be successful in their own right (and it doesn't always have to be career related—it can be your best friend who balances her work and personal life like a champ, or your mom, who is the kindest person you know). Watching them will help you more than you know.

Chapter 6

Heroes and Haters:
Learning Lessons from Other People

When I was a teenager, I looked up to Uncle Miguel's two sons. My cousins Mike and Rolando were pretty much ideal kids. They did well in school, respected their parents, and attended college (the first to do so from the part of the family that immigrated to the US). They both hold master's degrees in math from UCLA, which was my dream school, and which I still plan to attend one day. Though they were six and eight years older than I was, I still had every opportunity to follow their example. I went to the same schools they did and had a very similar upbringing.

Of course, as you know all too well by now, instead of following in their footsteps, I made all the wrong turns.

Mike and Rolando noticed and always tried to steer me back in the right direction, telling me I could do anything if I put my mind to it. They would frequently ask me about plans for my future and even offered to help me study and fill out college applications. I didn't listen, but they never made me feel bad about how I was acting and were never embarrassed by my behavior (which was good because I felt plenty embarrassed already).

Even though their attempts to reach out to me fell on deaf ears at the time, I did end up using their advice and guidance. Though it was not until much later, when I was actually ready for it, telling them that I was joining the army was my way of letting them know I was going to do something good with my life after all. They didn't make me feel less-than for taking a different road; instead, they provided me with support and reassurance that my future was going to be bright.

By the time I got to Iraq, Mike had become a high school math teacher and Rolando was a California Highway Patrol officer. I mean, come on—a teacher and a cop? Talk about making something of your life and helping to make the world a better place! I was just as impressed with their success as I was excited to finally be on the journey to find my own.

Other People Can Make You Better

As important as it is to be yourself and follow your own path, I never would have reached my full potential going it alone. I'm not saying you can't work by yourself or be independent and make your own decisions. All I mean is that other people have a lot to teach you—about yourself, about the world, and about the challenges that are sure to arise as you go along.

I can point to a lot of people without whom I wouldn't be where I am today—my mom and dad, who have always supported me; my sisters, who have always made me laugh, even in hard times; my amazing husband, Jesse, who is not only my life partner but also my business partner; and my viewers (of course!). But there are some key people who have ensured my success along the way. Some might not know the impact they had, some I've never met, and some have even taught me lessons the hard way.

Look around you—and you'll probably find examples of people you want to emulate. Figure out what you admire about them and try to do the same. This is different from copying someone else or not being yourself—it's about recognizing a quality or characteristic about them that inspires you. Maybe it's their confidence, their compassion, or their sense of humor. Maybe it's the job they have or the place they live. Try and think of yourself as a student at all times because there's always something new to learn. Use those traits you want to gain as the catalyst to drive you, to keep you going, and to get you one step closer to living the sweet life.

Get a Dose of Reality . . . TV

Starting anything new—whether it's school, a job, or even a business venture—is hard. By going out of your comfort zone and venturing into the unknown, you're taking a chance on yourself. That means the outcome depends on you and you alone. That's a lot of pressure! Throughout my career and the years leading up to starting my channel, I found comfort in knowing that no matter how daunting a new situation might seem, there was someone before me who had already been through it and had come out the other side in one piece.

I'm talking about role models and mentors. Let me clarify: While having both is equally important, there is a distinct difference between the two. Role models are people you look up to, or those living their lives the way you might want to live yours. You may or may not know them personally, but you have similar beliefs, values, and ideas. A mentor, on the other hand, can be a teacher, a family member, a boss, or an acquaintance whom you respect and admire. A mentor has already experienced what you are going through and has the knowledge to guide and prepare you for what comes next. In a professional environment, a mentor might even open a few doors for you or share some valuable contacts if you prove yourself to be a worthy mentee.

At different times in my life, I've been lucky to have both. Unfortunately, finding someone to mentor me through the first few years of my YouTube career wasn't really possible. When I started the Dulce Candy channel, vlogging was still considered uncharted territory. I was pretty much on my own when it came to figuring out how YouTube worked. There were a few others, like Michelle Phan, who were also doing it semiprofessionally, but blogging wasn't considered a bona fide business just yet. I agreed to some bad deals and made some not-so-smart business decisions because I didn't know any better and there wasn't anyone to advise me otherwise. Though I might not have had someone holding my hand and guiding my every decision, I was lucky enough to have someone I could look up to, a role model who provided me with valuable inspiration (and motivation!) when I needed it most.

As I've mentioned before, I was responsible for educating myself about fashion while in Iraq. So in addition to reading my magazines cover to cover, I'd watch certain TV shows that provided a glimpse into that world. One of my favorites was *The Hills*, which was huge at the time. Being stationed in Iraq, I was so far removed from life back home that the show really couldn't have come at a better time. It hit close to home on so many levels: It was set in Los Angeles, where Jesse and I were making plans to move after we left the army, there was a ton of fashion eye candy, and most importantly, it had Lauren Conrad, the show's breakout star. She was living the life I didn't even realize I wanted—interning at *Teen Vogue* magazine, attending the Fashion Institute of Design and Merchandising, and looking absolutely adorable while doing it.

Up until that point, going to school to study fashion hadn't even crossed my mind. Lauren was the one who inspired me to chase that dream. I have no way of telling whether I would have pursued an education in fashion had I not seen the show, but what I *do* know is that its positive influence on my life had a profound effect on my future and, consequently, my success. At that point in my life, Lauren was the perfect role model. Watching her on that show inspired me to e-mail Eva Chen, the beauty director at *Teen Vogue* at the time, to inquire about an internship. Even though life took me in a different direction with my YouTube channel and I never ended up applying for the internship, I'm forever grateful to Eva for taking the time to respond. I continued to closely follow Lauren's career, rooting her on when she started designing her fashion line, writing books, and growing her empire. All the while I took mental notes and made big plans of my own.

An important thing to remember about getting the most from your role models is that they're there to motivate and inspire you. You don't have to copy their styles or follow their careers step-by-step because no matter what, being yourself is still the best way to find success. Use the guidance and pointers you get from people you look up to, as tools you can use on your own journey.

LC isn't the only role model I've looked up to over the years. My Mexican heritage has always been an important part of my life and something I'm very proud of. I consider myself so lucky to live in a world where there are many strong, beautiful, and successful Latina women to look up to. Though there are many such women I could mention—Eva Longoria and Jessica Alba come to mind—one who needs her own special shout-out is Jennifer Lopez.

I've always appreciated J.Lo as a musician and a fellow Latina, but it wasn't until her appearance on *American Idol* that my admiration for her shot through the roof. I am constantly impressed by her confidence and work ethic. I know, I know: She's had years of being famous to practice, but still, you can't fake being yourself. Every time the camera lands on her she manages to be charming, hilarious, yet totally well spoken and humble. You can just tell that she is being 100 percent authentic.

When I started doing interviews, I had a very hard time feeling comfortable speaking on camera. From watching J.Lo, I learned that the best way to look good on camera is, in fact, to be yourself. I've never been in the same room as Jennifer Lopez, and yet I've learned so much from her.

Don't think that just because you're not already famous or wildly successful you have nothing in common with people who are. A role model could be a world-famous scientist or an award-winning singer; if they have qualities you admire, use them as inspiration.

Keep Your Role Models Close, and Your Mentors Closer

In addition to role models, you should try to find as many mentors as possible. As I said, mentors are like role models in that they are people you can look up to and learn from. The difference is that mentors are actually in a position to help you and counsel you one-on-one.

People often talk about mentors in a business setting, and it's common knowledge that you can find someone in your field who is a little ahead of where you are and ask them for guidance along the way. This is great advice, and if you know someone in this position who you think would be open to mentoring you, go for it.

But mentoring doesn't have to be that formal, nor are you limited to one mentor to help you, either. In fact, the more mentors you have, the better—that means you have a huge support network you can draw on whenever you need it, and in some cases, mentors can expose you to opportunities you wouldn't have had otherwise.

One of the greatest mentors I ever had was not someone I met in the beauty or vlogging world. He wasn't a teacher or a professional contact. He was a drill sergeant.

I already told you about Sergeant Johnson, the tough but kind man who taught me that breaking big goals down into little pieces would help me get better. But he did so much more than that. He would probably think it was funny that I considered him a mentor, so if you're reading this, Sergeant Johnson, SURPRISE!

Johnson separated himself from the other sergeants because he taught by example instead of just shouting orders. It's because of this hands-on, practical approach that I will always consider him a mentor. Being a drill sergeant wasn't just a job for him; he genuinely wanted us to succeed, and was willing to get in the trenches with us to make it happen. For the first half of basic training, I had dreaded the infamous five a.m. physical training test practice runs. They involved push-ups, sit-ups, and a timed two-mile run. That morning, rather than just stand on the sidelines in his work clothes like the other sergeants, Johnson came dressed in his PT shorts and Windbreaker, ready to run right along with us. I had completed the first two parts of the practice test and was close to finishing the run when exhaustion started to creep in. I still had two laps to go, and I could hardly catch my breath. Johnson saw me slowing down and quickly weaved through the others to run next to me. He started pointing out people ahead on the track and challenged me to push past them.

When I would reach them, he'd say, "Good. Now catch up to the next one." Every time I caught up to the person he pointed out, he'd point to the next one. While I was running, he'd motivate me by asking, "What's the worst that can happen? Your legs will fall off?" No, my legs didn't fall off, and with Johnson's help I finished the two miles with minutes to spare.

If you know someone who has taken the time to help you out personally, consider them a mentor and let them help you. Sometimes it's hard to ask for advice, or to know when you should seek help from others. With the right mentor, you might not even have to ask. Look for the people who want you to succeed, and pay attention when they give you advice. You may even find people in your own family, like I did with my cousins Mike and Rolando.

How to Handle the Haters

Remember Bethany? The girl I knew in elementary school who, despite calling herself my friend, took every opportunity to make me feel bad about myself? I thought I'd left Bethany behind for good as soon as I left middle school, but I still have to confront Bethany every day—this time in the guise of negative commenters on my YouTube page.

I am a positive person—I try to be kind and friendly to everyone I meet. I try not to judge people, especially before I meet them, and even if I have a negative thought about someone or something, I would *never* share it online. That's why I honestly cannot understand why so many people seem to delight in leaving nasty anonymous comments online. Didn't they learn that if you don't have anything nice to say, don't say anything at all? Apparently not.

You wouldn't believe some of the comments I get on my page. Sure, there are the typical negative comments about the videos themselves—especially in the early days when my technique was amateur at best. But on a daily basis I have people call me ugly and stupid and all sorts of other nasty stuff.

I hope you never have to face this type of abuse, but even if you're not bombarded with vicious comments, you can't escape negativity in your life. At some point, you're bound to come across someone who doesn't like you, or who doesn't think you deserve your success. This seems to become even more true the more successful you are—as you get more attention and recognition for your work, people will want to bring you down. The more people know who you are (especially if you're in a position of power—like a CEO or a politician), the more your actions will be subject to criticism. But I also bet a lot of the vitriol stems from something even more basic—jealousy. People who are extremely critical are unsatisfied with their own circumstances. I can promise you that not one hater is truly happy, fulfilled, self-aware, and busy with their own lives. If they were, would they be so consumed with yours?

No matter what, you can't let these negative people get to you.

Of course, unless you possess superhuman strength, ignoring the haters completely is virtually impossible. During the first few years of my vlogging career, a single negative comment had the power to ruin my day. Scratch that. Make that my entire week. As much as I had changed from the validation-seeking girl I was in high school, I still had my insecurities, the bulk of which stemmed from the fact that I was doing something pretty unconventional in my life and felt defensive about it.

Nowadays, I've learned how to manage my emotions, thanks to a few tried-and-true tricks I developed to handle the haters. The key is to spin their negativity into something positive. You can't control what other people say about you, but you can control how you respond. Getting upset or stooping to their level and hurling insults in the other direction will not make you feel better. In fact, if you do it in public or online, it could make people who once respected you turn against you. Here are my strategies for handling any haters that come your way.

Turn Mean Messages into Constructive Criticism

More than anything, the success of my business depends on my viewers' happiness. I wouldn't have a business if it weren't for the people who regularly return to my channel. Whether it's for a useful makeup tutorial, the discovery of a great new product, or an insight into my life that I haven't shared before, they keep coming back because I give them what they want. If I don't live up to their expectations, they'll stop coming back and my channel will be worthless.

Luckily, I have more than two million subscribers, and for the most part, they are not shy about telling me what they think. I used to fear the comments section—and avoided it like the plague! But I soon realized that the comments section is actually a powerful tool for gathering feedback about what my viewers want to see or, more accurately, what they DON'T want to see. Suddenly, reading the comments became a lot less stressful because, instead of taking critiques personally, I use them to gauge where there is room for improvement.

Sure, I have to weed through some not-so-nice words, but for the most part, even the unfavorable remarks hold a grain of useful information. If I look at negative comments as constructive criticism rather than a personal attack, I win on two levels: My confidence is left intact, and my business improves. The trick is to know what is constructive and what is designed to hurt. Also, know what you can and cannot change. If someone thinks I'm ugly, well, there's not much I can do about that. But if someone thinks my outfit posts are looking too one-note and I should try something new—that is something I might really consider.

Respond to Meanness with Kindness

We're all guilty of inadvertently taking our anger and frustration out on others. The difference is that most people feel bad about it instantly, while a select few get a kick out of causing others pain. More often than not, if someone calls you ugly, it has a lot more to do with the ugliness they feel inside than it does with you. So I like to give those viewers the benefit of the doubt and kill them with kindness.

If someone leaves a nasty comment nitpicking my appearance or a specific video, I respond with something I like about her. I may tell her that her hair looks pretty, that I like how she did her makeup, and that even though she may think I'm ugly, I think she is beautiful. And you know what? More often than not, she immediately apologizes! She goes on to explain that she's having a bad day, broke up with somebody, or had a fight with her parents and took it out on me.

The lesson here is that you never know what people are going through. They may have projected something awful onto you, but responding with negativity won't make you feel any better, and it certainly won't help them either. By responding kindly, you put the control firmly back in your hands and turn a nasty situation into an opportunity to make someone feel better. In the process, you may even turn that hater into a fan, someone who now sees you positively because you behaved so kindly toward him or her.

Don't Be Afraid to Delete

There was a time when I would take negative remarks way too personally, and the only way I could keep them from ruining my life was to disable the comments feature on my channel altogether. I've come a long way since then, and now I realize that the comments section provides way more pros than it does cons. However, I still implement a strict zero-tolerance policy when it comes to comments that are bullying or downright vicious.

There's a big difference between rudeness and straight-up hate. If someone threatens me, brings up my son or any member of my family, or addresses another viewer in a disrespectful way, I delete the comment and block the user without a second thought. I've always considered the people who subscribe to my channel my friends, and a true friend would never say something hurtful on purpose. If they did, that friendship would be over. The same rules apply to the comments section.

In addition to shutting out this kind of negativity from my life, I never want my viewers to feel like they have to defend me in the comments section (not that I don't appreciate them going out of their way to defend me, because I do!). If the Web gives you the power to literally erase even an ounce of ugly hurtfulness from existence, you'd better use that power! Don't be afraid to simply delete the negativity out of your life—out of sight, out of mind.

Don't Let Negative People Define You

One day, soon after my channel had started to take off, I received a hurtful comment I couldn't help but take very personally. In a response to a makeup tutorial, someone wrote, "Nice to see you're using your husband's money to buy makeup."

After we were both relieved of our army duties, Jesse was working as a security guard while I was making videos and deciding what to do next. As much as I wanted to write this person off as just another judgmental stranger who didn't know a thing about me or my relationship, the comment caused me to second-guess every decision I'd ever made: Should I forget my dream of attending fashion school and enroll in dental assistant school instead? Or was getting a degree from a community college and working a midlevel, nine-to-five corporate job the answer? Was I really just a shallow girl wasting her husband's hard-earned salary on useless things? And if I wasn't that girl, then who was I?

That, of course, was the question I needed to answer. But since I was struggling to define myself, I let a total stranger's thoughtless comment do it for me. After days of beating myself up, I logged on to YouTube to click through the comments section. The comment that instigated all this self-doubt was buried under dozens of sweet, supportive messages from my viewers. I decided then and there that I wasn't going to let a dumb—not to mention false—opinion take me down. The only one who gets to decide who I am is ME.

If you don't know who you are or what you stand for, there will always be people more than happy to tell you who they think you are or who you should be. This doesn't just apply to blogging. Negativity is an inevitable part of life, and it's up to us how we handle it. In letting other people's opinions color how I saw myself, I was missing out on getting to know the real me: a hardworking, kind, motivated woman who was well on her way to big things. Once I realized that, brushing off other people's hurtful words became easier. Of course, I get plenty of positive comments and encouragement from my viewers as well. But even though I love getting great feedback and knowing that people love my work keeps me going, I make sure to never put too much stock in those comments either. If you rely on others to provide you with confidence, you'll never learn to provide it yourself. Other people's opinions, whether positive or negative, became less relevant over time.

Chapter 7

Just Say No: Prioritize the Things That Matter Most

As soon as my YouTube channel started becoming successful, I got really busy really quickly. After so many years of dreaming about turning my passion for beauty into a career, I finally had steady work (and a steady income). But instead of being satisfied with what I had, and working as hard as I needed to to get my job done, I kept looking for even more to do.

For most of my life, I assumed that hard work had to be *hard*. Unless I was totally swamped and on the verge of burning out, I felt unproductive and believed that if I took a break, someone else would swoop in and take my job from me and therein would begin my decline into irrelevance.

This skewed perception of work came from watching my parents in their jobs. My mom and dad worked 365 days a year from sunup to sundown, and because they were my first example of hardworking people, I assumed that's what you had to do. What I didn't understand was they had to work so hard because otherwise they would not have been able to feed us or keep a roof over our heads. They had no choice—if they didn't work for an hour, they didn't get paid for that hour, and no matter how hard they worked one day, there was still more work to be done the next. Unlike me, they didn't decide what they did on any given day, nor were they doing something they loved.

Of course, my parents worked such long hours so that my sisters and I wouldn't have to, but at first, I took their example to heart, and even when I had a small nest egg saved up, I kept gunning for more work because I was afraid that the moment I stopped, I would no longer be able to provide the basic necessities for my family.

I also felt like if I wasn't working, I wasn't being productive. Having something to do all the time validated my purpose and made me feel in control. I needed to be a key player in every decision, or else people would think I didn't care.

Over the years, I've realized that one of the greatest advantages of having a successful career is being able to determine how much I work. The trick is, when you have control over your schedule, you need to make sure you actually exercise that control. Being busy is not the same thing as working hard, and if you work all the time, you'll quickly lose sight of the big picture—the priorities at work and at home that need to be given your full, undivided attention. Even though I was growing my channel in those early days, I was far from living the sweet life because I didn't have the capacity to actually enjoy what I was doing or make time for the other things in life that mattered.

In this chapter, I'll talk about the importance of learning to say no—to yourself, to others, to things that don't matter—so you can say yes with a full heart to the things that do.

More Is Not Always Better

As my YouTube channel gained more traction, my in-box overflowed with press releases, invitations, store openings, and new job opportunities. I had worked for months on my channel without knowing if anyone out there was really paying any attention to me, and this was a sign that I had made it. People were requesting my presence at raucous fashion parties, inviting me to do a step and repeat (where you pose on the red carpet in front of a banner) to celebrate a new brand, and even asking if I could represent their companies. It hadn't been that long since I had started making some serious dough with YouTube, so I jumped at every chance to go anywhere or to attach my name to anything.

Before I knew it, I was busier than a bee in spring. I was still spending most of my days shooting, editing, and posting videos, and at night I was going to events that I'd promised to attend, showing up at meet-and-greets I'd set up, or attending brand meetings. Ironically, while I was at my busiest, viewers started leaving comments about how lazy I was. I was offended. Couldn't they see how busy I was? Of course they couldn't. I had spent so much time focusing on so many different things that I hadn't spent enough time focusing on the thing that mattered most, the thing that had made me successful in the first place: posting quality and entertaining content that my viewers wanted to see.

I spent about a year juggling so many projects that I couldn't keep them straight. The thought of having an hour alone with nothing on my plate felt like a faraway dream. I hope you don't think I'm complaining: I'm so blessed to have these amazing opportunities come my way. My problem was that I was saying yes to just about every single one that did. I was running from one meeting to the next, and my channel started to become an afterthought. I didn't take the time necessary to focus on the foundation of my work because I was too distracted by shiny new opportunities. Therein lies the rub. I was dropping the ball on the most important part of my job! I am so thankful that my viewers called me out on it. Though at the time I desperately wanted my viewers to see that I was doing all sorts of work behind the scenes, but if I was honest with myself, I knew I wasn't putting my all into the videos. Soon, I would learn the difference between necessary and unnecessary work, and that hard work and working all the time are not the same thing.

On top of allowing the quality of my videos to slip, I remember a specific moment when I realized I was letting work get in the way of what is important. Luckily, it wasn't a major catastrophe: I didn't miss my son's birthday or forget about my wedding anniversary. It was a Saturday, and I had been working on editing a couple of videos that I planned to post the following week. I hadn't moved from my spot in my office in over five hours. The day had passed so quickly that I didn't even realize it was dark out until I looked up from my computer.

By then, Izek was itching to go do something fun, so, seeing how busy I was, Jesse stepped in and told me that he was going to take Izek to the ball pit at our local mall (Izek is obsessed with it!). I told them to have fun, and stayed behind to finish editing.

As I sat there in the dark with only the glow of my computer screen keeping me company, the regret hit me like a ton of bricks. I felt sick to my stomach as I imagined my son playing without me. I heard my conscience screaming, "This isn't what life is about!" I looked around at my empty house, eerily quiet without my family in it, and decided then and there that it was time for something to change. I waited until my family came home and closed my computer to spend the rest of the evening hanging out with them. The next time Jesse took Izek to the ball pit, I left my work behind to join them. I don't regret it for one second.

The Power of "No"

Life is about celebrating the small things and amassing simple joyous moments. Memories are not made by working all the time—and I certainly don't want my son to look back on his childhood and see a hole where I should have been. It was time to reprioritize. I was losing sight of all the wonderful things in life and I was too busy to realize it.

To find my fulfillment, I first and foremost stopped saying yes to everything. It was time for me to realize that working hard didn't mean working myself to the bone. I am the arbiter of my time. I used to rely on my work calendar as a way to schedule in other parts of my life. With this method, it was easy to push family appointments around because it meant that work took precedence. Now, I use our family calendar as my main scheduling tool. My work revolves around my family, and if we have a barbecue on the books, then I refuse the meeting that comes my way for that time slot. I've come to find that the people I work with are all extremely accommodating when it comes to family. I'm sure they all want to spend as much time as they can with their families, too (hopefully, this is the start of a shifting outlook about work in the US). I even bought a sign that's posted by my front door. I look at it every day before I leave the house. It reads, "Never get so busy making a living, that you forget to make a life." It reminds me to enjoy the fruits of my labor and to find joy in everyday things. My personal favorite way to enjoy my family? Walking to Rite Aid to get ice cream.

I've found that a large part of finding balance lies in choosing to do what fulfills you. I do one thing a day that makes my soul happy. This saves me when it comes to handling busy days at work. I usually spend time with my family when I need a break to recharge my mood and energy, but I also love to paint and listen to therapeutic music. Fulfillment doesn't come from proving yourself to others or making dizzying amounts of money. No, those are just fillers. True fulfillment means figuring out what "having it all" means to you. Does your "all" mean you find joy in exercising? Maybe it's finding joy in your work, in your family, in your friendships, in your city, or in your role in the world. You can get there by discovering the things your love, and making the time to enjoy them. Do the things that make you happy, and fulfillment will follow.

Carve Out Time for Joy

I'm beyond thankful that playing with makeup is my job. But, of course, there is stuff behind the scenes that isn't so fun (editing, scheduling, etc.). Even though I've found greater balance between work and my family, it's still important to have time for myself. Whether it's an hour a day or a weekend getaway, being a tiny bit selfish will make you a better spouse, parent, employee, and friend. First and foremost, you have to find what it is you love. Does the prospect of a quiet bath calm your frazzled nerves? Maybe it's traveling. Do you enjoy meditating, or going shopping with girlfriends? Or maybe the idea of staying in and reading a good book makes you giddy with excitement.

I love to meditate. I sit in a quiet area of the house and set my intentions. I visualize myself accomplishing the things I'd like to accomplish. Now, it's difficult to find a quiet place in my house or, frankly, a block of time for me to meditate. So I have to think of "my time" as mandatory time. Instead of waiting for a free moment that inevitably will never come, I schedule it into my day. Every morning before the rest of my family wakes up, I bring out a yoga mat, sit cross-legged in my office, close my eyes, and take a deep breath. When I create time to enjoy the thing I love, it helps me prioritize everything else. If it's something you love to do, you will undoubtedly benefit from indulging in it.

Work Belongs at Work

One of the most important lessons I learned from my parents was that one should take pride in one's work, even if it's not glamorous and especially if it's hard. No matter how exhausted they were after a long day in the fields, or how stressed they were about our finances (now that I manage a household, I understand that while we never wanted for anything, that doesn't mean it was always easy to provide for a family of six), they never let a hard day show on their faces.

It would have been so easy for them to succumb to self-pity, to complain about all the things they didn't have, to lament their decision to leave their home country in exchange for minimum wage and long days. But instead, they did what they had to do to take care of their family, and they did so with joy and humor.

Even though it took me a while to adjust to the idea that working hard doesn't mean working all the time, this is one lesson I still carry with me from my parents. No matter how stressed I get or how much work there is to do, when I'm spending time with my son, I never let it show. Not only does this allow Izek to enjoy the best version of his mommy that I can give him and to know that he is the center of my world, it also allows me to be present, to really spend time with my son and get to know him. That helps me be a better mother, and it also helps me relax so that when it's time to go back to work, I can do so without worrying.

Prioritize Yourself (Be Your Own Drill Sergeant)

It may seem odd to use the army as an example—a place where I had very little control over my own time—in a chapter in which I've been talking about the importance of asserting control over your schedule, but the army taught me that, when you are disciplined and don't make excuses, you'll be surprised what you can get done.

By the time I deployed to Iraq in September 2006, I'd grown accustomed to a super strict schedule. I was stationed at Camp Victory, Baghdad, one of the world's largest US military bases, where my daily wake-up calls were at 4:30 a.m. Music would blare through the speakers and jolt me and my bunkmates awake, indicating it was time for mandated physical training. Six days a week, I'd either put on my army-issued sweatshirt and pants (my physical training, or PT, uniform) and hit the gym for an hour, or switch things up and do a run around Camp Victory's lake. By 7:30 a.m. I'd be showered and on my way to the DFAC (the army dining facility) to grab breakfast. My workday began at 9:00 a.m. on the dot. I would take my post at the motor pool (the area where all the vehicles would park and where maintenance was performed) to spend up to fifteen hours a day working. Sometimes, I'd work for a full twenty-four hours straight before getting relieved, only to do it all over again a few hours later.

For the most part, I could not have been happier. Discipline seemed so hard at first (actually, it seemed downright impossible), but putting those rules into place for myself showed me that with a little hard work and organization, I could achieve things I had once thought impossible.

Though I left the army behind years ago, this discipline is the foundation for the life I have today. I make it a point to keep to a strict schedule. In order to do this, I need to know what my priorities are because that's the only way things get done. We've all been there—we have a free weekend, and instead of doing all the things we say we want or need to do, we sleep in, sit around, and before we know it, the day is over and we don't know what we've been up to. I hate that!

In basic training, our priority was physical fitness, and each of us had mandated physical exercise. We were required to be in bed and get up at the same time every day to keep us on schedule. This regimented schedule made for a much more productive day.

Today, my main priorities are my family, my job, and my own well-being, so I make sure to schedule time for all those things. Discipline for me means knowing my capabilities well enough so I can set realistic goals. I dedicate a certain amount of time each day to work and a certain amount of time to family. Because I know this going in, I know just how much time I have to accomplish a task and plan accordingly.

I also know that I get distracted easily, so I can't commit to doing one single task for very long. Instead, I work in bite-size chunks and schedule in breaks so I can stay focused when I need to and still get things done. It's taken a lot of practice, but over time I've come up with a routine that works well for me and leaves me feeling fulfilled without feeling frazzled.

I get up at seven a.m. and have breakfast. I break my weeks up into two sections: Mondays and Wednesdays are reserved for filming YouTube videos that I concept with help from my viewers. Tuesdays and Thursdays are reserved for editing. This way, my viewers can expect two videos a week. Sometimes I get more in, but I really try hard not to ever skip a week. I spend a lot of quality time with Final Cut Pro. I add music, graphics, and cut out the parts of the video that have lulls (or are just plain boring) to make the video exciting to watch all the way through. A fifteen-minute video can take up to five hours of filming and editing time (including some breaks along the way, of course)—when I am editing, rewatching, reediting over and over again, or re-filming lines that I keep flubbing.

Every morning, I make a to-do list of the tasks I need to achieve that day. Everything from my morning meditation to the videos I have to edit go on that list. No day is typical, so whether I need to shoot a video or set up for filming (fixing the white balance, adjusting the light and camera), it goes on the schedule. Beyond my work duties, I also keep reminders for the little things I need to do around the house like taking our two Pomeranians for a walk, making lunch for my son's field trip, or getting in a little exercise (I like to run or stretch). I do try to keep the list manageable because no matter what my day holds, my workday ends at five p.m.

After five p.m., my time is reserved for my son and husband. We have dinner as a family, play with toys, or just chat. This system helps me end each and every day with a sense of accomplishment. You likely have different priorities. Maybe you need to finish your homework before five p.m. so you can practice with your band before dinner. Or maybe you need to prioritize your time at the office so you can leave in plenty of time to make it to yoga class for that much-needed meditation. Whatever your priorities are, be your own drill sergeant and don't let yourself get away with breaking your own rules.

Know Yourself and Know Your Patterns

Another good way to keep your priorities in check is to find your patterns. It's easy enough to get distracted as is, but being in an environment that isn't conducive to your work style can make your day drag on and on and on. You want to find or create an area that is conducive to your best work. That way, you can breeze through, with as little distraction as possible (or maybe having a distraction every hour is what keeps you motivated). This comes with trial and error, but it's important to figure out what works for you. Is there a part of your house where you work best? Maybe you love sitting on the couch, or at your dining room table. Give a couple of places a test run and see where you feel the most productive. For me, my couch is where my productive days go to die. As soon as I sink into those comfy cushions, I'll start eyeing the remote control or the bag of chips we left on the coffee table from our last movie night. I will have suddenly lost hours watching a movie when I was just supposed to take a thirty-minute sitcom break. I've found that I need the rigidity of a table and a good solid chair to keep me motivated, so I work at my dining room table. It helps that there are lots of windows and sunlight to keep me feeling energized. I also know that I don't work well when I am feeling a little hungry, so I make sure to keep lots of healthy snacks on hand before I get started. Ask yourself when you get hungry, or even how many hours of sleep you need to feel your best. Some people are night owls and the only time they feel like they get anything done is when the rest of the world is asleep. Everyone functions differently, so be vigilant in trying to find what kind of pattern suits you.

Productivity: A Family Affair

Another way to amp up productivity is to celebrate even the tiniest victories. It can break up a monotonous week like a dream. In my family, we have our daily schedule posted on a chalkboard in the kitchen. Jesse and I must cross off the tasks we've delegated to ourselves that week, like editing, answering e-mails, or cooking dinner. Izek must do his chores, like picking up his toys and putting away the remote and video game controls in the living room. At the bottom of each day's family task is a reward that we've agreed on together—going to a movie, eating out at a restaurant, spending an evening at the park or on a family walk. When we finish our to-do list, we reap the reward (and if we don't, we get quite upset). Having these goals to work toward really helps us celebrate each day. But there's a larger victory here, too. Having concrete family goals makes us feel like one cohesive team. When we've accomplished our goal for the day and have rewarded ourselves, I feel connected with my husband and son the same way that a sports team feels proud of their win.

I've also implemented a mandatory shutoff time for my computer. This small act has had a big payoff. When I am disconnected from my work, I can shift my focus to my family. I've felt us get closer just by giving them my full attention. Before, I'd ask about my husband's day while skimming my in-box. Having my attention pulled else-where made him feel like he wasn't a priority, and truth be told, he was right. I wasn't making it my priority to pay attention. Even if I'm a couple minutes over my shutoff time, my son will come into my office and gently remind me. In the rare instance that I have an evening meeting that cannot be changed, I make sure to shut down at lunch, or block out an hour in my morning to hang out with my family. I remind myself that those e-mails will still be waiting for me tomorrow and that nothing major will change with an extra hour of work. But that extra hour of playtime? I've caught my son's first steps during that extra hour. If I had missed seeing him walk for the first time because I was answering e-mails, I would have been devastated. These small, pragmatic changes have helped improve the quality of my life immensely. It's helped me understand that if I work, work, work all the time, I may lose sight of what's really wonderful in life.

Chapter 8

When You're Not a Slave to Money, It Can Set You Free

There's a reason why my story of success only has one chapter that deals with the topic of money. It's because in the grand scheme of things, how much money you make is just one measure of success among many. I also measure my success by the opportunities it affords me to help my family, do what I love, and keep growing my business. Don't get me wrong, having financial freedom has given me the chance to see the world, guarantees that my son will get a great college education, and in general allows me and my family to live a comfortable life. And there's absolutely nothing wrong with reaping the rewards of your hard work. Your time and energy are valuable, and you deserve to be compensated fairly for them. The key is to treat money responsibly and think beyond the next handbag or pair of shoes to more substantial goals.

My attitude toward money wasn't always healthy. And like most things in life, it stemmed from my childhood and my struggles with self-esteem and insecurity.

For my parents, raising four girls on minimum-wage salaries wasn't easy. Money was always tight. We never had the electricity shut off or went to bed hungry—my parents always made sure we ate well—but luxuries like bacon with breakfast or fancy school snacks (the wealthier kids from the nearby naval base always had Lunchables, which were all the rage back then) were way above our budget. We got peanut-butter-and-jelly sandwiches, an apple, and homemade chocolate milk in a brown paper bag.

By the time I started high school, my mom had left her full-time job sorting onions. She was exhausted from the hard manual labor, so my dad was responsible for covering the majority of our basic needs—rent, electricity, gas. To supplement our income and make sure my sisters and I had new clothes for school (remember, my mom thought appearance was important for young women), my mom worked part-time as a cashier at Target. It was enough to get by, but perks like family vacations, cable, Internet (even dial-up), or lavish shopping sprees were out of the question. For a long time, back-to-school shopping consisted of trips to the Salvation Army. My mom would decide how many pairs of jeans, sweaters, and T-shirts each of us needed and then let us rummage through the discount bins for things we liked.

I was always aware that my family struggled financially. By the time I started high school I was so embarrassed by my thrift-store wardrobe that I begged my mom to at least take me to Payless for new shoes and to Ross Dress for Less, where I could find cheap stuff that wasn't previously worn by a stranger. I was constantly lusting after things other kids had: Brand-new K-Swiss sneakers, my own CD player (my sisters and I had to share one), and a beeper were all things I yearned for but my parents couldn't afford. The kids whose parents worked at the town's naval base weren't exorbitantly wealthy by any means, but their Converse shoes and electronic gadgets were a constant reminder of what my family actually could and could not afford.

I got a job manning the register at Hobby People when I was a senior, working the afternoon shift four days a week. My main goal was to get a car, which I did: a charcoal-gray 2001 Nissan Maxima. But there was no way to cover the lease payments, gas, and cell phone bills, much less all the clothes I was dying to own, making $6.25 an hour. My parents tried to teach me to prioritize. With each paycheck, I was supposed to figure out which of my basic needs to address first before I could indulge. For example: Does splurging on a new pair of shoes leave enough money for necessities like gas and lunch? If not, put a little bit aside from each paycheck until you've saved enough to cover the fun purchase while making sure the practical needs are met.

My parents tried their best, but few seventeen-year-olds—let alone ones plagued by constant insecurities like I was—are content being that responsible all the time. Since there was no way I was going to sacrifice my wardrobe for such unglamorous things as bills or lunch, I had to figure out a way to get my hands on more cash.

That's when Cynthia told me about credit cards (she may have been the most mature of all of us, but she also wasn't the best at taking our parents' financial advice to heart). She told me I could use the card to buy whatever I wanted, then make the minimum monthly payment of $10 to pay off the balance. What a deal, right?! I applied for a card immediately, and by the time it showed up in the mail, I was itching to take it for a spin.

It sounded too good to be true . . . because it was. When my parents saw that I had applied for a credit card, they warned me that interest adds up. As hard as they tried to stay on top of their minimum payments, some months were harder than others. They urged me to be responsible, to only spend what I could pay off. They warned me that debt was extremely difficult to get out of.

Of course, I didn't listen. After I got the card, I maxed out the $300 limit on makeup and clothes in a matter of hours. I knew I was responsible for paying off what I spent but treated the credit card as free money anyway. After a while, I realized my parents were right: Not only was it harder than I imagined to pay the monthly bills, but the interest rates made it feel like the minimum payments were barely making a dent in my principal.

Rather than face the music and figure out a way to pay my bills, I started to ignore the late notices. My parents explained that with a bad credit history I wouldn't be able to buy a house, a car, or even take out loans for college. But at that point in my life, things like college and owning a home seemed like far-off worries. Plus, if I couldn't afford to pay off a $300 credit card bill, how was I ever going to be in a position to buy a house? And college was out of the question anyway. By the time I got deployed to Iraq, I owed $1,500 on $300 worth of purchases.

The Best Thing Money Can Buy: Security

Let's recap where I was after high school, shall we? I was in a dead-end job with no hope of a future, having gone through a bad breakup that left me miserable. I had no close friends. I was drowning in insecurity and depression, and shopping for clothing and makeup was the only way I could forget about it all.

The only problem with instant gratification is that the joy and relief only lasts, well, an instant. Purchasing a pretty outfit felt great in the store, and the excitement might have lasted through the first time I wore it, but as soon as I hung it up in my closet, I was right back where I started, feeling lost and hopeless.

My bad spending habits stuck around longer than I care to admit, even after I managed to spend myself into debt at the ripe old age of seventeen. One of the perks of enlisting in the army is the signing bonus. After basic training, when I signed up for MOS, I received a $10,000 bonus simply for joining the military. It was like winning the lottery.

In between my MOS training in Maryland and deployment to Iraq, I was stationed in Fort Hood, Texas. This is where I went to work at the motor pool every day to train for my job as a driver on the convoy team for when I deployed. I was eighteen, on my own for the first time, and more important, I had money to spend however I wanted. As soon as I got the chance, I went straight to the military bank and withdrew the entire amount . . . in cash. I had never seen so much money in my entire life, and having it in my hands made me feel like I was on top of the world. I felt like I finally had the freedom to go into any store and purchase anything and everything I could possibly want, not on a credit card but with my own money!

My Iraq ship-out date was fast approaching, which meant if I was going to spend the money, I needed to spend it quickly. As I've mentioned, my shopping options in Iraq were limited, so to make sure I stocked up on everything I wanted, I made daily trips to the Fort Hood Target and the local mall. At Target, I filled up my cart with everything from notebooks and pens to bodywash and makeup to pillows and DVDs. Then I'd go to Forever 21 and Charlotte Russe for piles of flirty dresses, cute tops, and jeans. I was spending anywhere between $300 and $600 in a single shopping trip, and that's in addition to eating out every night. After years of struggling and feeling deprived, I felt that I deserved the freedom to buy whatever I wanted. My self-esteem might have been on the mend, thanks to basic training, but the second I felt the confidence boost from having a fat wallet, I wanted nothing more than to flaunt it. I loved the idea of *other* people seeing me pile my cart with tons of stuff and drop hundreds of dollars at a time. After years of feeling like the poor kid, I wanted everyone in the store—from the cashiers, to the stock boys, to the other shoppers—to think I was rich. I could have saved the money, but that wasn't nearly as much fun.

In a span of a month, the money was gone and all I had to show for it was a pile of stuff I had zero use for in Iraq. And the worst part? Owning all these *things* didn't make me feel any better about myself. I'm not one to dwell on the past, but boy, do I wish I had saved that money instead of mindlessly blowing it on junk.

In the military, salary is based on rank. During my time in Iraq, my rank as an E-4 specialist earned me $1,500 a month—not bad for a teenager. Since there was no need to purchase civilian clothes, pay for rent, or cook my own food while I was overseas, the money went far, and I was actually saving for the first time in my life. Thanks to this forced saving, by the time I got back from Iraq I had put away $11,000.

That money came in handy when Jesse and I moved into our own apartment off base. We were each making $650 a month at our army jobs and had to pay for rent, phone bills, and utilities. After what seemed like no time, I was right back to living paycheck to paycheck.

I can't begin to describe how mad I was at myself for spending my signing bonus so carelessly. For one thing, I would have been able to buy high-end MAC makeup, which I was obsessed with at the time, and I would have had more freedom to do fun things with Jesse. But more importantly, I wouldn't have had to worry so much about making each paycheck last to cover our needs. Good thing there were no emergencies during that time because we would have been in deep trouble. I had learned the hard way that spending money on material things only brings temporary satisfaction, but knowing that you have money saved up to pay your rent, provide for your family, or use in an emergency buys you the freedom from having to worry about all of that.

Luckily, Jesse was a bit older and had more experience living on his own, so he had a good handle on money management. He taught me to budget and organize our bills so nothing slipped through the cracks. But even though we were surviving, I couldn't help but wish we had more financial freedom.

Jesse also helped me pay off my credit card debt and even convinced the credit card company to forgive the astronomical interest charges I acquired while serving in Iraq. But the damage was done. My credit history was ruined. I couldn't lease a car, rent an apartment, or apply for a new credit card without having Jesse (he was very responsible with his finances and had great credit) cosign for me. For years to come, my bad credit served as a constant reminder to take my finances seriously.

I hope you don't have to make the same mistakes I did in order to learn how to handle money responsibly. This isn't a personal finance book, and even though I've learned a few lessons about money management, I don't pretend to be an expert. However, I do want to make this one point: The best thing money can buy is financial security. We've all felt the thrill of having a little extra cash to use however we want—even if it's just an allowance from your parents or a minimum-wage paycheck from your part-time job. And while I will never be the person to tell you that you shouldn't spend money on things you enjoy (how boring would life be if you never treated yourself?), you'll never be able to have a sweet life if you're always worried about money.

Don't get me wrong—I'm not saying that you have to be rich or have more money than you need. I'm just saying that, once you have enough money to take care of your basic needs, the happier you'll be. The more you save, the better you'll feel, knowing that if you need money for an emergency, it's there. Even though they didn't show it, I know my parents constantly worried about being able to feed our family and keep a roof over our heads, and I know it took its toll. Life is full of stress, so the less you have to stress about money, the better.

Trust me, I know it's hard, and I certainly don't want to preach to you about good money habits, knowing just how difficult it can be. The key is to get yourself into good spending and saving habits early so you don't make the same mistakes I did.

Earning Money Doing What You Love Is Way More Fun than Spending It

When Jesse and I moved to Los Angeles from Texas in January 2009, Jesse was looking for work while I was busy with my videos. Since neither of us was bringing in a steady paycheck, we were coming dangerously close to tapping out our savings. My channel was taking off, but I still hadn't figured out a way to make money from it. In fact, I was just hoping to become a YouTube Partner—an urban legend of sorts that existed among the vlogger community. Build enough followers, and YouTube would send you a paycheck every month. It was far-fetched, but I was chasing the dream.

That same month, I received an e-mail from *Seventeen*

inviting me to be featured in the magazine as a blogger to watch. I'd never done a professional photo shoot before, and had never even been to New York City.

During the shoot, I got to meet two other beauty vloggers. While we were chatting about vlogging, I mentioned that as much as I loved to do my videos, I needed to figure out a way to pay my bills, too. The vloggers were in shock that I wasn't making any money from my channel and asked me if I had checked off the YouTube revenue-sharing button. I had no clue what they were talking about. They explained that revenue sharing would allow YouTube to place ads on my channel and that I would make money off of those ads. I had no idea!

The second I monetized my channel, my videos were no longer just a hobby but an actual source of income. The first check I received from YouTube was for $3,000. The one after that was for $5,000. I couldn't believe that I was doing what I loved and actually making real money from it! I was finally making enough money to pay my bills, put some cash away for a rainy day, and still have enough left over to treat myself. My first instinct was to head straight to Barneys New York and Neiman Marcus on Rodeo Drive. My entire life I'd felt like I'd never have the luxury to go into a fancy department store without feeling like a poser. I felt destined to be broke and struggle because that's where I came from and I saw no way out. Having the freedom to go in and actually shop without maxing out a credit card made me feel like I had beat the odds. Shopping when I actually could afford to do it felt so much better than simply shopping to buy stuff and going into debt. Knowing that I was able to shop in my dream stores with my own hard-earned income was thrilling. And it wasn't because I was able to buy better stuff—it was because I knew that, for the first time in my life, I was financially independent. It seems like a lucky draw for me, and in some ways it was, but I wouldn't have checked off that revenue button if it weren't for that tip-off from my fellow vloggers. I should have done my homework, researched a little deeper, and tried to find out as much information about YouTube instead of waiting for a phantom partnership to arise. If I could turn back time, I would really invest more in making sure I was crossing my t's and dotting my i's. I would have talked to other people in my industry sooner. I would have reached out and asked the right questions.

How to Turn Your Passion into a Career

If you want to make money doing what you love, here are a few things to keep in mind along the way.

DON'T DO ANYTHING JUST FOR THE MONEY

Remember how I told you about the time, in a misguided effort to make my channel more profitable, I started seeking out opportunities based on how much money I could make? Remember how that backfired? When you use money to drive all of your decisions, you lose sight of your purpose, of who you are.

I started my channel because I truly loved making beauty videos. Even if I had never managed to turn it into a full-time career and resigned myself to fixing generators all day to pay the bills, I would still make them for myself. I honestly believe this attitude is what made me successful. If it's only money that is driving you, you won't find much joy in your job. And if you don't find joy in your job, you won't be very good at it. You'll probably do what you need to do to get by, but won't go above and beyond what's expected because you just don't care that much. Conversely, if you love your job, it probably won't feel like work. You'll be thinking about it day and night because you love it so much—and it won't bother you. You will get out of bed in the morning ready to start your day because you're excited to get to work. And because you love what you do, you will be good at what you do. And because you are good at what you do, the money will come naturally. When I started my YouTube channel, I definitely wasn't in it for the money. I just LOVED making videos. I was able to be myself and do what I wanted without having to compromise or answer to someone else (except my viewers, who weren't paying me!)—and the money followed shortly afterward.

RECOGNIZE YOUR WORTH

You know how people always like to tell you what kind of career you should have because you can't make money doing what you love? Few parents tell their kids they should grow up to be actors or musicians or makeup artists or acrobats because "There's no money in it! How will you survive?!"

Well, I'm here to tell you that if you work hard enough and have enough talent and people want to work with you, you can make a living doing pretty much anything. I get paid to talk about makeup all day. How is that possible?! There are literally people out there who make money playing video games all day, acting like they're someone else in front of a camera, creating sculptures with clay, or teaching babies yoga.

If you have a service to provide, people will be willing to pay for it. I'm not saying anyone can become a millionaire just because they have a quirky talent, but if you know what you're good at, you will be able to make money doing it.

The trick is to know your value. What service do you provide that someone would pay to have? What is unique to you and makes you happy when you do it? In my case, my videos are free so I don't make money off of viewers directly. But because I have so many subscribers, YouTube pays me for the opportunity to put ads on my channel. On the other hand, companies are willing to pay YouTube and me to put those ads up on my videos for those subscribers to see. It's like watching a commercial on TV. Understand your worth in the marketplace, and you'll understand how to make a living doing what you love. When those advertisers know they can reach a certain number of people, then they find what I do to be valuable to them. In other words, if it weren't for me, those companies wouldn't be able to reach a very segmented group of people so easily! My subscriber base and videos are worth something to those companies, as well as the companies who approach me to do events or promotions. If you love to hack computer code to make programs run faster, there is a job out there for you. If you love sports and could talk about it all day long, you are a valuable asset for someone out there. Even if it's an eccentric hobby or interest, you will be able to find a niche that values what you are worth. It's up to you to go and find it!

DO YOUR HOMEWORK

One day, early on in my YouTube career, I spotted an e-mail in my in-box that made me pause. The subject line read: "Personal invitation to New York Fashion Week."

Anyone who loves fashion knows that NYFW is where the crème de la crème of "it" girls gather, and I had only dreamed of rubbing shoulders with the likes of haute couture designers, models, editors, and world-famous makeup artists. I gasped out loud as I read the invitation. A potential collaborator wrote me a long (and very complimentary) e-mail asking me to be his date for a fashion show hosted by Ports 1961, a venerable fashion house that specializes in luxury apparel. They were throwing a huge show, and this collaborator had an extra ticket with my name on it.

I e-mailed him back immediately, accepting his offer. I started thinking about what I was going to wear (my favorite black dress and sky-high heels) and the beauty looks I wanted to try (contour and bright lips).

As I was dreaming up my street-style-shot-worthy look, I saw a response back from the man who had invited me. In this follow-up e-mail, he outlined his terms. He would not pay for my round-trip flight or the cost of my hotel room, and there was no budget for any meals. His once-friendly tone became cold and calculated as he laid out the time that we should meet in front of the fashion show entrance. I was so enamored of the idea of going to New York for the first time (and with a golden ticket no less) that even though my gut told me something was fishy about this offer, I agreed. Most of the vloggers I knew went to NYFW in collaboration with a brand as part of a marketing strategy. Some would get a flight, others a hotel stay. This collaborator made it seem like we would be working on a business opportunity together where I could leverage my social media following in exchange for this brand-new, very cool experience. I had no reason to think that he had other ideas.

When I landed in the Big Apple, I was envisioning lots of flashbulbs, parties, and, well, New York glamour. What I saw was a hectic and stressful situation where editors and bloggers are basically shepherded to and from shows with lots of air-kisses and cigarette smoking in between. The hotel I booked was some twenty blocks away from Bryant Park, and hailing a cab was nearly impossible: They were all claimed by women looking to rest their heel-clad feet. I was in my own pair of platform monstrosities and, because I didn't know any better, decided to walk from my hotel to the fashion show.

When I got to the Ports tent (drenched in sweat, with hot, painful blisters forming on the heels of my feet), the man who was supposed to be my "business contact" handed me a ticket and nearly pushed me out of his way to go schmooze with some C-list actresses who had gathered in front of the tents.

I was grief-stricken. I was shocked. I was also out hundreds of dollars. I slunk to my seat, smack-dab in the middle of an obscenely long row. I felt suffocated as person after person filled in the empty chairs on either side of me. The business "collaborator" didn't say a word to me as he took his seat and the lights dimmed, and then bolted out of the tent as soon as the last model walked the catwalk.

This was a huge lesson for me. Not every opportunity

that comes your way is a good one. There is a way to recognize good and bad opportunities, and the only way to do that is to do your due diligence. First and foremost, listen to your gut. Is it telling you that something doesn't add up, or that an offer is too good to be true? Oftentimes, your conscience is loud—it's just a matter of whether or not you listen to it or tell it to shut up. Second, ask questions. Ask as many questions as you can about the ins and outs of an offer, what the expectation of your role is, and what benefits you'll garner for contributing your time/energy/money. And last, don't agree to anything until you get something written down on paper and are comfortable with the terms of the agreement. As cringe-worthy as my NYFW experience was, I think back to it whenever I am offered a new opportunity or project to remind myself to look at the projects, parties, and partnerships that come my way with a more discerning eye. It is shocking to see the number of bad opportunities I probably would have said yes to had I not had that NYFW experience. Now I can come to the negotiating table feeling confident that I have all my ducks in a row.

Just like you're the only person who can manage your time, you're the only person who can manage your salary. Sure, you may not be able to get whatever you want, but if you feel as if you're being shortchanged or not getting a fair shake, speak up. A lot of times, people don't like to talk about money, but the only way to know if you're being treated well or taken for a ride is to ask direct questions. If someone is honest, they'll be up front with you. And remember, just as you should never do anything simply for the money, you should also feel free to turn something down if it's a bad deal.

GIVE BACK

Being able to help others is the best reward for success. Once I had a little bit of a nest egg saved up, the first thing I did was start helping my parents to pay them back for all the sacrifices they made for me. It is, to this day, one of the most gratifying things I've been able to do. You don't have to give away huge chunks of your income to give back. My journey on YouTube has been a huge blessing, and I've been learning a lot about my purpose here on earth. I've discovered how impactful this platform is when it comes to helping others. One viewer reached out to me about her brother who was diagnosed with leukemia. She wanted to partner with me in the hopes that I could help her get the word out and help her family attract monetary donations. Just knowing that my channel has the power to help others feels pretty darn good inside. And I'm proud to say I've helped out a few families this way. Pick a cause that's close to your heart (for me, that's St. Jude's Children's Research Hospital and World Vision) and make a monthly donation of whatever amount you are comfortable with—every little bit helps! It doesn't have to be just money either—it can be your time when you want to volunteer, or donating stuff that you no longer have a need for that others might want. Give back to your own community. Whether it's a food bank, an animal shelter, or the Boys and Girls Club, the gift of your time is the best gift of all.

One of the ways I try to give back is to mentor my nineteen-year-old sister, Wendy Teresita. I've found that donating your expertise can be hugely beneficial, too. Everything I've learned along the way, I now get to share with her because, believe it or not . . . she's vlogging! Though her channel is about beauty and makeup, just like her big sister's, Wendy sets herself apart by doing fun DIY tutorials, like making bronzer out of cinnamon and mixing homemade hair spray out of sugar and water. How awesome is that?

I take my mentoring responsibilities very seriously; Wendy Teresita might even say a little *too* seriously. I helped Wendy figure out a publishing schedule so she could stay organized and provide her viewers with consistent, quality content. I remember how hard it was to be nineteen and figuring out my next steps, so I do my best to encourage Wendy to do what she loves and follow her heart. You undoubtedly have your own unique set of skills. Take a beat and think about what it is that you're good at. Do your friends come to you and ask you to help organize their closets, or teach them a recipe for your amazing dishes? Maybe they ask you to fix their computers or change a tire? You have knowledge that others deem important, so spending a little time sharing it can be immensely fulfilling—even beyond a monetary donation! Giving back to an organization or community you care about helps you get out of your own universe for a little bit and is a good reminder that there is a great big world out there that you're contributing to.

Chapter 9

Don't Settle When You Settle Down: How to Find the Perfect Partner for Your Life and Your Work

As my career grew, it became clear that the best thing for our family was for Jesse to become my business partner. He could have had his own full-time or even part-time job, but my channel was providing more opportunities than I alone could handle. I am the face of the business, but Jesse is a huge force behind the scenes. He left his old security job and joined the Dulce Candy brand full-time as an all-in-one key decision maker, administrator, IT guy, production lead, chief operating officer, project manager, and photographer. He also shoots all the content for my website and channel, but most importantly, he's my support. In essence, he helps the business run smoothly, whether that means setting up the lighting for a video or dealing with partnerships. In November 2014, we also launched a new channel, Izek's World, which features Izek and Jesse's father-son adventures. So now the business is a true family affair!

You may not work with your significant other, but he or she is still a partner when it comes to your career. Even if you don't have a job in common, and even if you do vastly different things, the person you spend your life with can make or break your success. That's not to say you *need* someone else to be happy; success and happiness can absolutely be found on your own terms. But your partner will have a huge impact on your work.

A supportive partner can affect your confidence, your self-worth, your attention, your energy, and your vision for the future. Someone who can impact these areas of your life in a positive way not only is integral to your happiness, but also contributes to your ability to achieve the things you want to achieve. It's hard enough to do it on your own, so would you rather be with someone who encourages you to keep going, who helps you when the going gets tough, who is happy for every victory you have? Or would you rather be with someone who keeps telling you he (or she) doesn't get it, that you should give up, that your idea is stupid and bound to fail? Or even someone who is lazy and doesn't help you when you need it? The answer should be clear.

Think about what success means to you and then ask if

there is room for a partner in that equation. Is there room for someone who fits into your idea of happiness and success? There's no reason to find a partner for partner's sake. No, instead, you want your partner to make every aspect of your life better. That's not to discount romance and love—of course those are important, too. But between all the lovey-dovey stuff, there needs to be a deep mutual respect and support of what the other wants to achieve for him- or herself as well. Your partner will not only be your sounding board but also the person you spend every day with, so their choices will affect yours and your choices, theirs. You need someone you can rely on, and you yourself need to be someone reliable as well.

The Right Person Will Make You Feel Good about Yourself

Jesse and I met when we were deployed at Camp Victory in Iraq. It was a tough time, and we were both going through bouts of homesickness. We met through mutual friends, and after weeks of superficial greetings, we sat next to each other in the DFAC at dinner. We quickly found out that we had a ton of stuff in common, including the fact that we were both from California, and both children of immigrant families.

That dinner turned into a late-night conversation and then, from there, a recurring meeting. We would wind down our days together, and spend hours talking in our spot at the DFAC. We talked about everything: from our shared favorite ice-cream flavor (mint chocolate chip) to our hopes and goals for when we left the military (I didn't have any clue yet, and he wanted to do security work, maybe).

But what we found in each other was more than a shared love for really good ice cream. We found a support system that would ensure success for both of us. For so many years I had been with losers who didn't care what I thought or did. They didn't care if I succeeded or failed. My first boyfriend, Michael, had done a number on my self-esteem. How can you feel good about yourself and take pride in your self-worth if your own boyfriend doesn't think you're important enough to be treated with common decency? But in Jesse, I found someone who believed in me whether I wanted to sell Mary Kay or I needed some time to figure out what my next steps were going to be. He fell in love with me when I told him about my ambitions. He helped me set up the camera for my YouTube videos and was my shoulder to cry on when I wanted to give up. Instead of letting me, he'd push me to be better and to try attacking my problem from another angle. He made me feel smart and was always impressed by the ideas I had. He made me feel supported. I relied on him when the going got tough.

Make Sure You Have the Right Goals

The other reason I knew that Jesse was the one for me was because we wanted, and still want, the same things for ourselves and our family. We both loved kids, and we were both devoted to taking care of our parents as they got older. We had the same political beliefs, and both have a heart for adoption. We had shared dreams of living in Los Angeles, where we would be close to our families and hometowns, and were both big fans of discipline (we did meet in the army, after all).

Sometimes great people don't make great couples because they don't have the same goals. Even if you meet someone and you just click, and he makes you feel great about yourself, you may have different desires and goals for your lives that aren't compatible. Maybe you want to get married and start a family right away, but he wants to travel the world before he settles down for good. Or maybe he wants to live close to where he grew up, and you want to move to the big city so you can take your career to the next level. If something is really important to you, don't give it up just to make someone else happy.

Of course, that doesn't mean it's "my way or the highway" every single time. Relationships require sacrifice, and you need to be willing to bend to make things work and to tackle any challenges that arise. But there's a difference between giving

up a major life goal and something that's a minor want—
maybe you wanted to take a romantic vacation with your love,
but he got a huge promotion and had to stick around for work.
It's okay to compromise in the short term as long as you're on
the same page when it comes to your long-term plans.

You Can't Change People, But People Do Change

If you and your partner want different things out of life,
you can't assume he will change his mind down the line
and you will live happily ever after. However, people do
change and the person you settle down with when you're
twenty may be very different from the person you're with
at sixty. If you settle down with someone, you need to understand that you will both change as the years wear on.
You will not be the same person you were at fifteen when
you turn thirty, so be open-minded and, hopefully, your
significant other is just as open-minded as you.

Jesse and I have been together for eight years. We started
dating in our early twenties, so growing and maturing as
individuals became an inevitable part of our relationship.
But change doesn't have to be a scary thing. In fact, I've
learned to relish it because change means that there is another
challenge on the horizon (and let's face it, as scary as a challenge may be, that's how you grow).

I'll be honest: There was a time when both Jesse and I were going through so many changes that it felt as if we were leading separate lives. I realized that I hadn't looked him in the eyes for weeks, even though we shared the same home, had meals together, and were raising our son together. To fix this, I decided to start small by making more eye contact and instigating conversation. Just a little eye contact could remind us that our worlds were bigger than ourselves and that we had each other to thank for our home, our loving son, and our fulfilling jobs.

I had changed a lot since we'd started dating, and I realized I'd never taken the time to consider that he had as well. It scared me to think I didn't really know who my husband was anymore, so I started at the beginning and asked him the questions you'd normally ask on a first date: "What's your favorite song?" and "What is your dream job?" I thought he loved hip-hop and that his dream job was, well, forever working on the Dulce Candy brand. But, surprisingly, he answered every question differently than I thought he would. I learned that his favorite band was actually Led Zeppelin—a far cry from N.W.A. and Wu-Tang. I learned that he loves John Lennon and old-school rock. I learned that he was interested in astronomy and wanted to someday try his hand at becoming an engineer. I was getting to know him all over again, and it was very exciting!

It didn't surprise me that he had changed—any person would over the course of nearly a decade—but I was shocked and disappointed in myself that I didn't know who he had changed into. Simply asking questions is a great tool for keeping the lines of communication open. If you start to grow apart or feel disconnected, these simple changes can make a huge difference in helping you reconnect and become solid partners again. That way, you change together, and reevaluate the goals that you've set for your relationship and yourself.

Be Mindful and Listen

When Jesse had a full-time job and I was trying to work on my YouTube channel, he'd come home from work, and as soon as he'd walk through the door, I'd bombard him with requests. I would ask, "Can you wake up early tomorrow with me and take pictures of my outfits?" I'd suggest that if he had a little extra time he go through some of those e-mails and respond for me because I was still editing videos. Jesse, being the saint he is, would let out an exasperated sigh, but go straight to sifting through my in-box and preparing our DSLR camera for an early-morning shoot.

Jesse didn't have the heart to tell me that he hated doing vlog-related work as soon as he stepped foot through the door exhausted from work. And because I was so busy and focused on growing my channel, I didn't bother to ask him if he *minded* helping me. Nor did I offer to return the favor. After a few months of this, Jesse had had it. All of a sudden a simple conversation about work blew up into a heated argument. I felt as though he was being unsupportive, and he felt the same about me. I thought that, because he was supportive of what I was doing, he should be willing to bend over backward to give in to all my demands. I thought that, because I was so busy and my channel was taking off, and he wasn't as busy, he should want to pick up some of the slack.

I was forgetting that he had his own priorities and needed time to himself. This was a turning point in our relationship, when I asked him to leave his full-time job to help me grow the business. He still has dreams of one day being an engineer, but for him, a short-term compromise is worthwhile for his family. He thought about my request for a couple of days, and when he told me he decided it would be best if we both devoted all of our energy to growing the YouTube channel, I was ecstatic. He himself had found working from home attractive and the channel needed the manpower, so we found a solution that helped us both achieve what we wanted to do. We worked toward a common goal that fulfilled both of us.

Now, of course, going into business with your significant other is not for everyone. But there are ways to apply this to your life. The important thing is to remain teammates whether the goal is to save up for a house or a vacation or to raise your kids in a certain way. Pay attention to your partner's needs, desires, and limits, and if you feel he's not paying attention to yours, let him know in a nonconfrontational way. Don't let resentment boil over before it's too late. If you have the right partner, you will find a solution.

Fight Fair

Fighting is inevitable no matter how great your relationship is. Life is stressful, things don't always go as planned, and we're all human and bound to have a bad day or let emotions get the better of us. Sure, if you fight all the time you might want to reevaluate if he or she is the right person for you. But don't assume your relationship is bad just because you fight sometimes.

The trick is to fight fair. It's not how often you fight but *how* you fight that should gauge the health of your relationship. If there is a mutual respect and validation of your significant other's feelings (whether you think you're right or not), then both parties can come to an agreement. Fights can even clear the air as long as both parties are willing to think of the argument as a learning experience, rather than a competition.

I used to think that, for every fight, there was a clear winner and a loser. The person who lost was the one who apologized first because, in my mind, saying "I'm sorry" was the same as saying "I was wrong and you were right." Now I realize that sentiment is incorrect.

If you and your teammate are working toward the same thing, then "winning" a fight doesn't mean that you haven't backed down. The only way to win a fight is for both parties to come away feeling they've had a productive, logical, and insightful conversation. Winning means finding a solution that works for everyone. Now, I consider saying "I'm sorry" as a sign of maturity. Listening to someone else, even if you think he or she is wrong or overreacting, is a sign of respect, and maturity means you know how to set aside your pride and end a fight. I learned this from years and years of fighting—I've had lots of practice! But again, that's not a bad thing as long as my husband and I both feel like we've been heard. Fighting fair is one of the hardest things that someone can do, but being with someone who challenges you can help you mature and grow as a person.

The Roller-Coaster Theory: Lows Lead to Highs

I consider my parents a shining example of a great relationship. They have experienced so much stress and hardship throughout their thirty-year marriage—including two years apart—but instead of letting that tear them apart, they worked together to make their marriage strong and rode out their lows together.

I think it's important to have an example of a long-lasting marriage in your life. If it's not your parents, it can be a family member's marriage or a friend's parents' marriage, too. That's not to say that every long-lasting marriage is a healthy one; a healthy one is strong enough to ride out the lows and get to the highs again. One of the greatest lessons I have learned is to say "I'm sorry" when I know I am wrong. I used to let my ego get in the way, and my pride wouldn't let me say sorry. At one point in my teen years I even said to myself, "I will NEVER say sorry." Now, as soon as I regret what I say, I apologize and tell him why I said that. Our relationship is a lot healthier because we both recognize when it's time for something as simple as an "I'm sorry."

I've also realized that finding the right partner means having someone who will stay with you through the lows. When I didn't take the red carpet CoverGirl job and was moping on the couch, it was Jesse who helped me see the other side. He told me that if I'd taken the job, I might not have been as successful at it as I could have been if I had felt 100 percent comfortable with the situation. He's held my hand while I cried over horribly mean comments on the vlog. And it's been Jesse who has celebrated with me when we hit four million views on our most-watched video (the Lady Gaga tutorial). There are weeks where I look at Jesse and feel an overwhelming sense of warmth and love. And there are weeks where I am so busy that I just need to be alone to get my work done. There will inevitably be times when we are hitting it off great, and days when there is a misstep at every turn. But we've celebrated the hardest when the other gets a win, and mourned the deepest when the other goes through a loss. Having a teammate makes the roller coaster a less terrifying, more thrilling experience.

Chapter 10

Beauty from the Inside Out

Beauty is my career and has always been a huge part of my life. Without makeup and fashion, I wouldn't be where I am today, and you wouldn't be reading this book. But even if you're not in the beauty industry, or if you're not all that into fashion and style and don't like wearing a lot of makeup, beauty is still critical to your success.

No, I'm not saying you have to be dressed to the nines, stay current with all the latest trends, and perfect your makeup every morning in order to be successful. Beauty is more than what you put on the outside of your body. It's about how you feel about yourself on the inside. And if you want to live the sweet life, you have to feel good about yourself.

Have you ever noticed that the most beautiful people in

the world aren't the best-looking people—rather, they are the most confident people? When you see movie stars out on the red carpet, they look like they deserve to be there, like they know they look good and aren't afraid that everyone is watching. You can slather a woman in makeup and put her in a Versace gown, but if she's cowering in the corner, what's the point? At the same time, some women can wear a burlap sack and no makeup, but their smiles light up a room and their confident posture makes you wish you could look exactly like them.

Real beauty is not about how you look on the outside but about how you feel on the inside. But as you know by now, it took me a long time to really adopt this mantra and apply it to myself. When I was younger, I spent a lot of time obsessing over my outward appearance. Whether it was big, bouncy hair, painted lips, the cutest outfits (complete with skintight jeans and midriff-baring tops), or the trendiest bags, I relied on the superficial to make me feel good about myself. I was so obsessed with the physical definition of beauty that finding out who I was on the inside wasn't a priority.

I believed that I could only feel beautiful if I had access to all the makeup and clothes that would make me look beautiful. But when my YouTube channel started taking off and I finally had access to tons of beautiful clothes, the latest accessories, and all the big-name makeup money could buy, I realized I was just as insecure and unhappy as

I had been when I was a teenager. It wasn't what I put on my body that made a difference; I had to fix what was inside. I couldn't *feel* beautiful until I *believed* I was beautiful—that I was smart, confident, and had something important to offer the world. It occurred to me: How could I put myself in front of millions of people every day and talk about beauty when, deep inside, I didn't believe I was beautiful? How could I be a role model to the young women and girls who looked to me for advice if I wasn't truly proud of myself?

Now that my relationship with outer beauty has changed and I no longer define myself by how I look, I've come to appreciate beauty for what it really is—something that comes from within but is projected on the outside. When you feel good about yourself, makeup and clothes become even more powerful because they allow you to augment the image of yourself you want the rest of the world to see. They become a way to express yourself and play up all the things that make you special. Therefore, I want to spend some time talking about how feeling beautiful can prepare you to take on the world.

See the Beauty That Others See

Who in your life makes you feel beautiful? Your parents? Your best friend? Your boyfriend? We all have moments when we don't feel especially beautiful, but chances are, someone thinks you are. I don't know why, but it's human nature to get hung up on our imperfections instead of focusing on our best attributes. You may have gorgeous almond eyes, but you can't stop thinking about how you wish your thighs were slimmer. Or maybe you have a beautiful smile but think no one can see it next to your problem skin.

You are your own worst critic, and I have found that, more often than not, no one notices your imperfections more than you do. So when you're feeling low, think about how the people who love you look at you.

For me, that person is my mom. She has never judged me or made me feel silly for feeling insecure. Instead, she'd talk to me like a friend, and when I felt at my worst, she'd tell me that even though I didn't look like a supermodel on the cover of a magazine, I was a different kind of pretty, my own special brand of beautiful. To a mother, her child is the epitome of beauty—even his or her imperfections can't take away from a mom's unconditional love.

So throughout the course of the day, rather than bash my appearance or get down on myself for feeling self-conscious, I started to feed myself the same positive affirmations I'd give my own daughter if I had one: "You are talented, you are honest, you are funny, you are smart, you are kind." My husband compliments me on my hair, so I take extra good care of it. My son loves stroking my skin and holding my hand, so I use lotion every night. My mom tells me she loves my eyes (they're just like hers, so of course she loves them), so I love to wear eye shadow and eyeliner to play them up. Sure it takes time to learn to love yourself, but acknowledging the things that other people compliment you on is one place to start. Once I learned to allow myself to accept those compliments and enhance the features that my loved ones loved about me, I felt more confident in who I was both inside and out.

Ask yourself, "Who in my life makes me feel special and beautiful?" Is it your mom or dad who tells you how proud they are of all you've accomplished? Is it your little sister who tries to be like you and dress like you (as annoying as that sometimes seems)? Is it a teacher who commends you on a job well done? A friend who always gives you a shoulder to cry on? Think about how that person makes you feel and then start treating yourself the same way they treat you. Most of us would never talk to someone else the way we talk to ourselves. Would you ever tell your best friend she was ugly or stupid or not good enough? Of course not, because you love her. So why do you say the same things to yourself? Once you change the conversation, you'll change how you see yourself and the world.

There Is More than One Way to Be Beautiful

As a teen, comparing myself to the stunning models in *Teen, Cosmopolitan,* and *Seventeen* magazines gave me a very unrealistic notion of what being beautiful meant. While marveling at a model's flawless skin and sculpted body, I was very aware that I looked nothing like her. Back then, I had no way of knowing about the amount of work and re-touching that goes into making a model look the way she does in magazines. All I saw was the finished product, so I was looking at myself through a totally unrealistic lens.

Every woman is unique and therefore has distinct re-quirements for what she needs to feel good. What makes you feel beautiful or sexy can be a million different things, and it will most likely be different from what makes someone else feel beautiful. I suggest starting by pinpointing your fa-vorite physical attribute. I happen to think I have great legs. I may be short, but my legs are lean and muscular, which is something I keep in mind when I want to feel extra con-fident. I'm fairly conservative with my personal style but have no problem showing off my legs with a short hemline. Play up what you love, whether that's your super strong nails, your pearly whites, or your collarbone. Next time you find yourself prepping for a hot date or a fun girls' night out, think about what you like most about yourself and make it a point to show it off! And even if you have some parts you aren't entirely jazzed about, there's no need to hate on yourself for it. I'm a firm believer in playing up what you love, and downplaying what you don't. I like my legs, so I will don a skirt. I think I could use a couple of inches in the height department, so I invest in good, comfortable heels to help give me a little lift. Doing so can be a small way to build big confidence.

Arrogance and Confidence: Two Different Things

When was the last time you declared, out loud, that you were beautiful? While we're encouraged to embrace femininity and work on our self-confidence, there's a stigma attached to openly talking about our appearance in a positive light. Too often, we worry about coming across as arrogant and thinking we're better than everyone else. And, yes, it can get obnoxious when someone goes on and on about how hot she is all the time (we've all met that girl—or that guy!—who thinks she's God's gift to humanity). But that's not what I'm talking about.

There's a difference between being conceited and being confident. Women should—yes, I'm saying it—feel proud of how they look! Not only that, we should have the freedom to voice it without being accused of arrogance. If you feel beautiful, you should be able to scream it from the rooftops!

Start by catching yourself when you have the urge to put yourself down and turn the negative thought into a positive one. If you think you're having a bad hair day, compliment yourself for having the ingenuity to try a new style. If you think those bags under your eyes make you look exhausted, remind yourself that you're a hard worker and those bags under your eyes are a result of how brilliant you are at your job. Once you get that down, start giving yourself positive affirmations while you're getting ready for work or school. Tell yourself you're beautiful as you put on makeup, admire how that dress accentuates your feminine curves, and set a positive intention for your day.

I first noticed the line blurring between "confident" and "conceited" in the YouTube comments section. If I said something about liking the way I did my hair or appreciating how I looked in a new outfit, viewers instantly labeled me as "stuck-up" or said I was "thinking too highly of myself." And it's not just online; the same double standard applies for women on TV and in film. Confident ladies who love their bodies and own their beauty are often written off as selfish, bitchy, and egotistical, especially by other women. How often have you said of another woman—famous or not—"She's so full of herself" or "She tries too hard" or "She looks fake"? This can't be right!

Instead of putting one another down for accepting and liking our own appearance, we need to encourage each other. If you think someone is beautiful, telling her can go a really long way to boosting her self-esteem. The concept of "girl power" is all about women supporting one another and sticking together. Making one another feel beautiful is an important part of that process.

Want to take matters into your own hands? Here's what I propose: Next time you find yourself with a group of girls—no matter where you are—take an opportunity to boost their self-confidence. We've all been there: One girl points out something she doesn't like about herself—be it her thighs, her hair, or her nose—and all of a sudden there's a chain reaction of insecurity. The next girl feels like she has to say something negative about her own appearance in solidarity, then the one after her, and so on. Before you know it, a casual hangout turns into a full-on self-bashing session.

Don't be afraid to reverse the cycle! Take control of the situation and casually steer the conversation in a more positive direction. Compliment a friend on her outfit. Tell her that her shade of lip gloss looks great and that you think her new glasses make her look smart and sexy, not at all dorky. Or better yet, muster up the courage to say something complimentary about—wait for it—yourself! Your courage may give your friends the go-ahead to say something positive about themselves.

Women shouldn't feel embarrassed to openly appreciate their own beauty. Start a cycle of positivity within your group of friends and see if it catches on. Just watch; you'll start feeling better about yourself, too.

Also—and this is important—if someone pays you a compliment, the only appropriate response is to say "Thank you" and mean it. Someone is being nice to you, so accept it and appreciate it! Why do so many women feel the need to argue when someone compliments them—"Oh, you like this dress? You don't think it makes me look fat?" There is nothing arrogant about taking a nice remark at face value.

Powerful Women Embrace Their Femininity

Confession time: Before I joined the military, I kind of took being a girl for granted. Sure, I relied heavily on all the obvious things that came with the female territory—playing with makeup, obsessing over clothing and shoes—but I didn't understand the power of femininity until it was stripped away from me completely in basic training. As I explained before, both men and women are not allowed to enhance their appearance in any way upon entering the military. Applying even a single coat of mascara or nude nail polish was a big NO-NO.

The rules eased a bit after basic training, and I was allowed to wear makeup—within regulation, of course—and even get acrylic nails (they had to be clear and couldn't be too long). Having even the smallest freedom to tap into my girliness made me yearn for it on a whole new level.

By the time I got back to the States, I was starved for all the things I had been deprived of during my service. My first outing was a shopping trip to the closest mall for trendy civilian clothes, followed by a luxurious trip to the nail salon. From that point on, I made sure to infuse as much of my life as possible with feminine touches. Working in the motor pool, I still spent the bulk of my day in uniform, so I took great care to always have a fresh manicure and spent a chunk of my morning carefully applying makeup and putting up my hair into a neat bun.

The evenings were all about getting dressed to the nines in my new clothes and going out on the town. Well, sort of. Killeen wasn't exactly a cosmopolitan city, so I was forced to improvise. The second I got home from work I would jump in the shower and get all dolled up in a cute outfit, heels, and elaborate makeup to go to, wait for it ... Walmart! Not the most glamorous destination, but I was grateful for any and every chance to get out of my uniform and into something stylish. I finally had an opportunity to show off my personal style, and I wasn't about to pass it up, even if I was just aimlessly wandering the aisles of a discount superstore. I wanted to dress up for myself, and myself alone. It made me feel so much better about myself to enter into the world looking great. It's not about trying to impress others, as a matter of fact; it is just about feeling good.

Am I saying that you, too, should dress yourself to the nines in order to go buy toilet paper? No. I dressed up to go to Walmart because it made me happy. When you look good, you feel good. What does that mean for you? Maybe you wear makeup to the office but can't wait till the weekend so you can hang out in your bare skin au naturel. Or maybe you like to wear makeup around the house—even if no one but your dog is going to see you all day. If it makes you feel good, it's worth it. Don't let anyone tell you otherwise.

These days, getting dressed up is still important to me, but I treat it as more of a luxury—something I look forward to as a reward for working hard. Whether it's date night with my husband or a fancy event, I consider getting ready a special occasion, too; the actual process of picking out an outfit, styling my hair, and applying my makeup is all part of the experience for me. Being a mom, I can't wear heels while chasing after Izek and running around for meetings, school pickups, errands, and work. And to be perfectly honest, there is so much filling my days that I simply don't have time to go all out with my look. That said, staying in touch with my femininity is still very much on my list of priorities because I feel my best when I do.

My goal is to avoid getting too comfortable while still maintaining my active lifestyle. I work from home, so unless I'm shooting a video or attending a meeting, I could easily get away with spending the day in my pajamas. Add that to the fact that I've been in a relationship for the past eight years, and it would be totally understandable if I paid less attention to how I present myself. But to do that would go against everything I've come to believe and appreciate about my own femininity. Staying consistent about little things that help me feel sexy and beautiful every day is the key to maintaining my overall well-being. Even on my busiest days, there are a few things I always make sure to do:

Keep It Neat—Even if I know my day will be spent at home working on behind-the-scenes stuff, I always make sure to brush my teeth and shower. It sounds silly, but you'd be surprised how easy it is to put off such mundane details when there's no chance you'll be stepping outside. Even if the most glam events on my agenda are grocery shopping and a casual dinner with my boys, I always make sure my hair is brushed. And instead of doing crazy makeup, I'll pick a pretty lipstick along with a cute casual outfit.

Wear Cute Undies—Whether I'm rocking sweats or a ball gown, I always make sure that my bra and panties are pristine. Let's clear something up right away: This has nothing to do with whether anyone actually sees my undergarments. Wearing cute lingerie is my right as a woman, and I intend to use it. I stock my underwear drawer with cute bras and panties because they help me feel sexy even on the busiest of days.

Maintain a Mani/Pedi—This one is left over from my army days. I've grown to really appreciate how good it feels to have well-groomed nails. It doesn't mean that I need my nails painted a wild color, and it certainly doesn't have to be done at a salon, but it's a tiny detail that has the power to make a big difference in how I feel about myself. What little things make you feel beautiful?

Stand by Your Choices

....

I got breast augmentation after having my son at twenty-three. I never had large breasts, so when I became pregnant, having my bra size jump from an A cup to a C was a very pleasant surprise. I loved having curves and the boost of confidence they gave me. I felt more in touch with my femininity than ever, which in turn made me feel powerful.

After breast-feeding Izek for two months, I was left with a bust that was even smaller than it was before I got pregnant. The truth is, I missed my womanly curves! For me, going under the knife was all about embracing my femininity. I loved feeling proud of my body during pregnancy and knew that getting a breast enlargement would give me that feeling permanently. So I went for it! And I don't regret it for a second.

Two years after my breast enlargement, I got minor rhinoplasty. The decision to do it also stemmed from wanting to feel more feminine. I see shaving down the tiny bump on the bridge of my nose as the equivalent of getting braces or working out to lose weight: It's a way of taking action to enhance your appearance; it doesn't change the way you feel on the inside. Plastic surgery isn't brain surgery; it has zero effect on your emotions or how you view yourself. You are the only one who has the power to change that.

Two months after I got rhinoplasty, I posted a video on

my channel titled "My Plastic Surgery Story." It garnered almost two million views and over nine thousand comments, making it one of the most popular videos I've ever posted. About 85 percent of the comments were supportive and understanding. People said even though they thought I looked beautiful before, they respected the choices I made about my own body as a grown, confident woman. Some even went so far as to say they respected me for acknowledging that I had work done when I could have easily gotten away with not mentioning it at all.

The remaining 15 percent who didn't agree with my choices were downright scathing. I was called "plastic" and "fake," and even accused of being ashamed of my Mexican heritage—the absolute furthest thing from the truth.

Some may think the reason I shared my plastic surgery story was because I felt the need to defend myself. Yes, I always want to be 100 percent honest with my viewers, but I don't owe anyone an explanation for my personal decisions. That said, I'm glad that by talking about it, I was able to open people's minds even a little bit to the fact that not every reason to alter one's appearance is an unhealthy one.

Popular belief is that unless it's medically required, getting plastic surgery is a sign of low self-esteem and general unhappiness with one's appearance. While there are definitely cases in which that might ring true, I consider my plastic surgery a success because I did it for the right reasons. My main goal for posting that video was to give my younger viewers a different perspective—one that I hope will help them understand you can't depend solely on your appearance to make you happy. Altering the way you look doesn't change how you feel about yourself. You don't magically start to love your body if you surgically enhance your breasts. You don't gain instant confidence if you fill out your lips or change your nose. All those things come from inside, and no amount of surgery will change that.

A Healthy Body Is a Sexy Body

Have you ever seen someone who was out of shape, stressed, tired, or strung out and thought they looked sexy? Doubtful. It's imperative to take care of yourself, both mentally and physically, if you're going to be your best self. This can mean different things for different people, so find what's most important for you and focus on it. If movement and music make you feel your best, then carve out time in your hectic schedule for biweekly dance classes. If it's preparing healthy meals at home, then invest in a cookbook and teach yourself some new recipes. For me, staying active and maintaining a balanced diet are a must. I notice a negative change pretty much instantly if I slack on my fitness routine. I become grumpy, sluggish, and much more susceptible to stress. And quite frankly, the positive results—loads of energy, clearer skin, and general strength—far outweigh the short-lived bliss of skipping a workout in favor of downtime on the couch.

That's not to say that I'm a strict gym rat. Not even close! For one thing, I don't do intense workouts every day. Instead, for the sake of keeping things interesting, I break up the week with different activities. Three mornings a week are devoted to the T25 program at home. Technically, you're supposed to do these super intense workouts six days a week, but my focus isn't to lose weight—just to relieve some stress and get my endorphins flowing. On other days, Jesse and I drop off Izek at school and go on a hike. We are lucky to live in an area that's home to tons of nature parks and hiking trails, and I do my best to take advantage of them.

Because I was raised on some of the most incredible homemade Mexican food, I've always had a love for it (this explains why I was on the chubby side in high school). The traditional Mexican dishes my mom cooked regularly were delicious, hearty, and nourishing, which is why I will always consider food a source of joy and comfort. But when I joined the army, I also learned just how important proper nutrition is for general well-being. Without maintaining healthy eating habits, it would be nearly impossible to keep up the levels of activity that were required of us. These days, I'm nowhere near as active as I was in the military, but I still make sure to give my body the nutrition it needs to tackle the day.

My Daily Diet usually goes something like this:

Wake up: 1 glass of cold water, 1 cup of coffee with regular creamer and 2 cubes of sugar.

Breakfast: Alternate between steel-cut oatmeal and a homemade whole wheat breakfast burrito with sausage and eggs. One glass of orange juice (fresh-squeezed if I have time).

Lunch: Turkey sandwich on whole wheat bread with mayo, lettuce, and tomato and 1 glass of iced tea. I'm not too picky about what I eat at photo shoots or lunch meetings, but I do make sure to add some form of protein to my salad or sandwich to keep my energy levels high.

Snack: Cold veggies like carrots or cucumbers with fresh-squeezed lemon juice and a dash of chili powder. I also whip up a quick fruit salad of watermelon, strawberries, and cantaloupe (depending on what's in season). If I'm really hungry or craving something warm, I make a baked potato and sprinkle it with lemon juice and chili powder.

Dinner: Brown rice with veggies and grilled chicken or pork. On cold evenings and time permitting, I make a hearty chicken soup using my mom's recipe.

Dessert: I don't have a sweet tooth, but if I'm craving a sweet treat, I'll have a few bites of ice cream with Izek, or a cupcake.

I end the day by taking a multivitamin to make up for any nutrients I missed out on.

As far as dieting goes, I believe that life is too damn short to deprive yourself of what makes you happy! So if you want to indulge in something that's not necessarily healthy (my weakness is Spicy Sweet Chili Doritos), go for it! Just like everything else in life, maintaining a happy and healthy lifestyle is all about balance.

Style Secrets for the Sweet Life

When you're busy running a business, raising a child, going to school, or being just plain swamped, a uniform (both beauty and wardrobe) can help save your sanity. Then, you only have to use brain space for the details, whether it's a swipe of red lipstick, a fresh mani, or a crazy-cool haircut that will amp up your overall look with minimal effort. After some major tuning, I've amassed a stable of go-to beauty tricks that make me feel great. It starts with good grooming, where the basic idea is to put your best foot forward every day. Here are the steps I take in both my makeup and wardrobe that make me feel like the best version of me.

WHERE TO SAVE AND WHERE TO SPLURGE

I used to think that expensive = better. But even now that I'm in a position to afford name brands and pricier items, I only like to spend money on things that are actually worth it. I've found that there are certain things on which it makes sense to splurge, and others where it's fine to scrimp a bit.

Save

1. *Mascara:* There are beauty-editor-loved formulas that you can buy for a song at your local drugstore, like cult favorite CoverGirl LashBlast Mascara. That famous hot-pink-and-neon-green bottle sells for under $10.

2. *Manicures/pedicures:* Getting a manicure can be a luxury, but it can get expensive fast. I give myself manicures at home and go through a pampering process that lets me feel like I'm not missing out.

That includes a bowl of warm soapy water, really good lotions and oils, pushing down my cuticles, filing the nails down to the shape I want, and fun music turned on in the background.

3. *Basic clothing:* I've never spent over $30 on a T-shirt. I don't ever want to feel precious about my clothes when I'm running around chasing my son (spaghetti doesn't scare me when my outfit doesn't cost as much as my mortgage payment).

4. *Foundation:* Name-brand foundations are very, very expensive, and you're paying for their marketing. I've found my favorite foundations on the shelves of my neighborhood drugstore, and there's hardly a difference in formula. I love Revlon, CoverGirl, and Almay.

5. *Makeup brushes:* You should avoid the super, super cheap synthetic stuff (the bristles can be rough on your skin), but there's no need pay an arm and a leg either. Midrange makeup brushes from your local Target are really great quality tools. I like Sonia Kashuk.

Splurge

1. *Shoes and bags:* There are two schools of thought: Splurge on clothes or splurge on leather goods like

shoes and handbags. I am of the latter school.
Good-quality shoes and bags can last a lifetime,
and their resale value stays high over time. Even
expensive clothes get worn out and go out of style
quickly. Plus, the cost of dry cleaning can end up
being more than the cost of the item itself!

2. *Coats:* I usually buy one good coat every couple of
years. If it's a quality one, it'll pay for itself wear
after wear after wear.

3. *Skin care products:* Moisturizers, cleansers, and
creams. My skin is the backbone of my business, so
it's important to invest!

4. *Jewelry:* I buy important, timeless everyday
jewelry pieces so that I can pass them on to my
family one day.

5. *Hair:* There's nothing quite as awful as a bad dye
job. It takes a lot of time and money to keep up
colored hair, so if you're going to do it, make sure
you're willing to commit to it before starting.

6. *Under-eye masks:* Find your one trouble spot and
invest. For me, it's dark under-eye circles. I throw
my wallet behind some pretty pricey eye masks,
but it makes a huge difference.

For the Mane Event

1. *Find an awesome hair mask.* People don't often think beyond the shampoo and conditioner, and I personally never thought it was important to use a mask. But if you frequently use heat tools, using a mask will make a difference right away. I buy mine from my local drugstore. Make sure that you buy the appropriate formula for your hair type (look for categorization on the front of the bottle).

2. *The women of the past knew* what they were doing when they spent their nights in curlers. The best way to get volume (for those of us with longer hair) is with Velcro heat rollers. Wrap your hair around a couple of these and place them on the crown of your head, and fifteen minutes later you have sky-high hair. If it ain't broke, don't fix it.

3. *Find a hairstylist you trust.* I experimented with a ton until I found "the one." She knows my entire hair history, and knows exactly what I like, with minimal explanation. Once you find your go-to person, you'll never leave the hairdresser's chair only to cry in your car ever again.

Get Glam

1. *I have lots of compacts and palettes:* eye shadows, blushes, powders in hundreds of colors. The most annoying part of pressed powder makeup is when they inevitably break and crumble. The powder gets everywhere! For an easy fix, add a couple drops of rubbing alcohol into the powder, cover with a piece of plastic wrap, and press down firmly with a quarter until the powder is packed back into the pan. I've saved many a palette this way.

2. *I live in California,* so a sun-kissed glow is standard fare. To fake it, use your favorite bronzer to brighten up your face. Start at the top of your forehead and apply in a number "3" formation, moving from your hairline down toward your temples, under your cheekbones, and ending on the jawline. Repeat on the opposite side of your face.

3. *To make your lips appear fuller,* take a pearly highlight shimmer and dab on the center of your bottom lip and also in your cupid's bow (the dip right above your upper lip). Finish with a gloss around the shimmer and blend inward. Instant lip plump.

4. *Eye makeup remover can be expensive.* I use organic coconut oil instead. Just melt onto skin in a circular motion and then wipe off with a tissue or

baby wipe. (Other uses for organic coconut oil: lotion, hair oil, and even an antiseptic on small cuts)

Skin Deep

1. *My biggest tip for skin care:* Test products until you find the ones you love. Stay loyal to them until your skin type changes with age or for other reasons. Your skin likes consistency!

2. *When you find that your makeup doesn't* go on as smoothly, reach for a mask. When you use a face mask, don't let it dry completely. (It'll tug at your skin and can cause wrinkles.)

3. *Lastly, do not lie out in the sun. I repeat:* DO NOT LIE OUT IN THE SUN. I know having a natural tan may seem cute, but I promise it's not worth the brown spots, wrinkles, and potentially scary skin diseases later on. You can always use bronzer (see makeup tip above) and a good self-tanner to get equally glowy results.

Bodywork

1. *Have a nighttime ritual* to let your mind know its time for bed. After my nightly shower, I spritz one

spray of perfume behind each ear. It instantly relaxes me and helps me get ready for a good night's rest.

2. **You may find your favorite product** in the most unusual place. Be open to it! Bag Balm has been a lifesaver for my feet. It's a salve that was originally created for farmers to use on their cow's udders after milking, but I swear that my feet have never been softer.

3. **Exfoliate your skin every other day.** I like sugar scrubs with oil that you can buy at your local drugstore. The extra benefit is that the oils hydrate your skin so that you can skip lotion after your shower or bath.

Primp and Prime

1. **Tweezing your eyebrows** should be left to the professionals. If you're desperate to go at it, please resist the urge. Your first go-around should be done at a professional brow spot (or at least done by someone you trust who knows what she's doing) so that you have a guideline. Then, use the professionally done guideline to get rid of the strays as they grow in. If you mess them up once, they'll never grow back the same. Ever.

2. ***Moisturizing your cuticles*** can prevent infection, and conversely, picking at your hangnails can lead to one. Keep them healthy and hydrated, and no picking!

The Perfect Uniform for Any Occasion

As a busy mom and business owner, I've narrowed down the uniforms I reach for when I get dressed. Having a go-to look for any occasion will not only ensure you look great no matter what, but it will also save you a lot of time and energy trying to pick out what to wear. I rely so heavily on them that they've become second nature for me. To keep them feeling fresh and new, I circle in some seasonal trends, too. I've broken them down on the next few pages.

· LOOK 1 ·
Everyday Daytime

When comfort is key and running errands is on the agenda, I rely on easy basics that let me jump from parent car pool to video editing. I feel most like myself when I'm dressed like this.

Hair: I'll usually tie my hair back into a ponytail or a bun. As a mom, I don't have a ton of time to style, so this is my go-to do.

Makeup: BB cream (an all-in-one sunscreen, foundation, moisturizer), mascara, bronzer or blush, and gloss.

Clothing: V-neck T-shirt, skinny jeans, flats, cardigan.

· LOOK 2 ·
Creative Work/Business Meetings

I'm well aware of the space I'm in, so I try to stay current and modern with trends. Keep in mind that my guidelines work for a creative field.

Hair: I make my hair straight and sleek. It's timeless and still professional.

Makeup: I work in beauty, so I have to make sure that my look is in line with current trends without going over the top. That means mascara, false eyelashes, winged eyeliner, medium-coverage foundation, bronzer, highlighter, and a pink lip (all with a light touch).

Clothing: Boots, jeans or leggings, tunic, topped off with a blazer. I showcase personality through accessories like necklaces, earrings, and bracelets.

· LOOK 3 ·
Media Appearances and Important Events

I go all out for media appearances and red carpet events. That means using a heavy hand because makeup can get washed out in photos or on video.

Hair: I use extensions for maximum volume and length and love to wear loose curls.

Makeup: Neutral, soft browns on the crease and shimmery highlight on my brow bone, false eyelashes, concealer, highlighter, blush, powder, bronzer for contour, lip liner, lipstick, eyeliner, mascara, eyebrow pencil; and I finish with a setting spray so that it lasts all night.

Clothing: I'm petite, so I like A-line dresses that give me the appearance of a waist. And of course always, always heels.

· LOOK 4 ·
Weekend

My weekend plans usually include something a little bit more fun. I love to go to museums with my family and will usually choose a look that is something between everyday work and business.

Hair: Worn down, air-dried.

Makeup: BB cream (an all-in-one sunscreen, foundation, moisturizer), mascara, bronzer or blush, and gloss.

Outfit: Chambray top, floral print shorts, brown booties, satchel, accessories like necklaces, earrings, and bracelets.

Conclusion: Keep Dreaming

So here I am: a loving mom, wife, daughter, and CEO of my very own thriving YouTube business, one I've built from the ground up with nothing more than drive and sheer will. I have legions of followers I'm lucky enough to call friends rather than fans, and a slew of big-name brands knocking on my door for a chance to collaborate. Oh, and I've written this book—my greatest accomplishment yet! Pretty impressive for someone who just a few short years ago didn't think her story was that interesting, much less inspiring.

It took years of hard work to get to the place where I felt my words might actually be able to help other women. It took conquering all manner of fears, insecurities, and obstacles. It took diving into my past and mining it for valuable lessons. It took me realizing that past mistakes don't define the person I am today. It took major soul-searching, stumbling, and getting back up again, only to find that my joy was right in front of me all along—I just wasn't ready to see it yet. Once I was ready to accept it with arms wide open, it became crystal clear that the only thing standing in my way was me.

At this point, you might wonder what's next for me and the Dulce Candy brand. Am I finally ready to call it quits and enjoy the fruits of my labor? If you've learned anything about me from this book, you can probably guess that the answer is a big, fat, resounding NO! And though I'd be lying if I said I didn't seriously consider taking a breather, I don't think I have it in me to ever stop moving forward. Not only that, I don't think I'd ever want to. I'm proud of my success (these pages are proof that I worked damn hard to get it), but I never want to feel like there's nothing left for me to work on. Besides, I have a pretty massive to-do list to get through.

Number one on the list, and most definitely the obvious next step, is to launch a cosmetics line. But not just any cosmetics line! I've worked hard to establish my brand and just like anything that bears the Dulce Candy name, the line has to meet my standards. For one thing, it needs to be up on all the latest beauty trends, feel luxurious and top quality, yet not cost my customers an arm and a leg. I'll never forget what it felt like to walk through department store beauty counters and lust after the pretty packages of lipstick, eye shadow, and blush only to walk out empty-handed because I couldn't afford a single thing. I may not have my plan of attack mapped out just yet, but the idea is ready to go, and I know I have it in me to grow it into something tangible.

Then there's my ongoing mission to spread a message of positivity, confidence building, and self-love. While this book was a very important and far-reaching first step, it's still just the beginning. I want to take things to the next level outside my YouTube channel with large-scale motivational speaking or casual in-person meet-and-greets. I know that the community of unique, beautiful, inspiring people I've built over the years will help me get there. And after that's all done? Who knows! Maybe it's growing my family, going back to school, or writing book number two. The possibilities are endless.

Just look around you! Every single day has the power to bring with it new inspirations and ignite your creativity if you're willing to be open to it. More than anything, I hope that reading this book helped you see your own potential and inspired you to always be on the lookout for new and exciting opportunities. I pray that you never stop believing in yourself, that you keep your heart and your eyes open, and that you accept life for the beautiful journey it is. There will always be struggles along the way, but you have the strength to get past them while still enjoying every precious moment. While you're on your journey, treat yourself with kindness, love, and respect and extend the same treatment to those around you. And most importantly, never ever stop dreaming, always reach beyond your goals, and never be afraid to take a bite out of the sweet life. You deserve it.

Acknowledgments

First and foremost, I would like to thank my husband, Jesse. You are my partner, my best friend, and my soul mate. Thank you from the bottom of my heart for supporting all of my decisions and sticking with me through both the good times and the bad. I'm so grateful that you constantly push me to be the best person I can be. You always put our family's needs first, and as I always tell you, we are blessed to have a wonderful man like you in our life. Izek and I LOVE you!

I want to thank my mom and dad and my sisters Cynthia, Yvette, and Wendy for supporting me. Dad, you're the best promoter! Mom, I couldn't get through life's obstacles without your wisdom and advice. And to my sisters: You guys are a blessing. I thank God every day for giving me the best of friends as sisters! I'm lucky to have all of you in my life and I love you all so much. And, Wendy, thank you for always lifting my spirits when I'm down and being the best sister anyone can ever ask for. You are so unique and you're never afraid to be yourself—I have always admired that.

acknowledgments

To my other family, the Ruiz family, thank you for welcoming me into your hearts eight years ago. You have been there with supporting and open arms and I truly appreciate it.

To my management team, you guys came into my life and took my career to a whole new level. I am forever grateful to you for always believing in me. Thanks for caring about my family and making us a part of *your* family.

Petar, you inspire me as a human being. You are a great example of someone making a positive difference in this world just by living your life with honesty and integrity. I admire your intelligence, kindness, and heart. Thank you for always working so hard for all your "kids" and making our dreams come true. You've also been a great contributor and a huge help during the writing process—believe me, it never went unnoticed.

I would also love to thank Diana Ryu and Kate Wolfson, who have played a vital role in the birth of this book. Thank you, ladies, for dedicating so much of your time and passion to making this book a reality. I honestly can't thank you enough! Gratitude for support is also owed to my amazing and loving book agent, Eileen Cope, my entire team at Penguin, including Brooke Carey, Caroline Sutton, Megan Newman, and everyone else who has worked so hard and believed in my story. And to Stephanie Horbaczewski and the whole team at Style Haul, you saw something in me six years ago that helped me become who I am today.

acknowledgments

Last, but not at all least, to my YouTube friends—calling you viewers or fans doesn't feel entirely right because you guys are so much more to me than just a screen name. You have shown me what girl power is all about. Thank you so much for being with me since 2008; we have been living this adventure-filled journey together. I have grown and learned so much through these seven years and I want to thank you for growing with me. I am so grateful for the unconditional support you provide for every endeavor I embark upon. Your letters and e-mails touch my heart and I know that even though I may not have the pleasure of meeting every single one of you in person, we will always have an unbreakable bond.

I would also love to thank the following ladies for supporting me through all these years: Pricilla, Irene, Yola, Morgan, Angie, Kara, Tara, Marissa, and Reyna—your combined strength as women is truly amazing.

Thank you to my big boy, Izek, for showing me what love *really* is, for making me laugh with your silliness, and for connecting me with God. I hope I make you proud. Never forget that I love you and that Momma will always be there for you.

Xo,
Dulce